Access 2013:
Intermediate
Student Manual

MOS Edition

Access 2013: Intermediate

Chief Executive Officer, Axzo Press:	Ken Wasnock
Series Designer and COO:	Adam A. Wilcox
Vice President, Operations:	Josh Pincus
Director of Publishing Systems Development:	Dan Quackenbush
Writer:	Steve English
Keytester:	Cliff Coryea

Trademarks

ILT Series is a trademark of Axzo Press.

Some of the product names and company names used in this book have been used for identification purposes only and may be trademarks or registered trademarks of their respective manufacturers and sellers.

Disclaimer

We reserve the right to revise this publication and make changes from time to time in its content without notice.

ISBN 10: 1-4260-3661-2
ISBN 13: 978-1-4260-3661-3

Printed in the United States of America

1 2 3 4 5 GL 06 05 04 03

Contents

Introduction

*Add coloumns
and fields -*

Access has tables .

Inner joint .

Outer joint .

*One to one
One to many*

After reading this introduction, you will know how to:

A Use ILT Series manuals in general.

B Use prerequisites, a target student description, course objectives, and a skills inventory to properly set your expectations for the course.

C Re-key this course after class.

Topic A: About the manual

ILT Series philosophy

Our manuals facilitate your learning by providing structured interaction with the software itself. While we provide text to explain difficult concepts, the hands-on activities are the focus of our courses. By paying close attention as your instructor leads you through these activities, you will learn the skills and concepts effectively.

We believe strongly in the instructor-led class. During class, focus on your instructor. Our manuals are designed and written to facilitate your interaction with your instructor, and not to call attention to manuals themselves.

We believe in the basic approach of setting expectations, delivering instruction, and providing summary and review afterwards. For this reason, lessons begin with objectives and end with summaries. We also provide overall course objectives and a course summary to provide both an introduction to and closure on the entire course.

Manual components

The manuals contain these major components:

- Table of contents
- Introduction
- Units
- Course summary
- Glossary
- Index

Each element is described below.

Table of contents

The table of contents acts as a learning roadmap.

Introduction

The introduction contains information about our training philosophy and our manual components, features, and conventions. It contains target student, prerequisite, objective, and setup information for the specific course.

Units

Units are the largest structural component of the course content. A unit begins with a title page that lists objectives for each major subdivision, or topic, within the unit. Within each topic, conceptual and explanatory information alternates with hands-on activities. Units conclude with a summary comprising one paragraph for each topic, and an independent practice activity that gives you an opportunity to practice the skills you've learned.

The conceptual information takes the form of text paragraphs, exhibits, lists, and tables. The activities are structured in two columns, one telling you what to do, the other providing explanations, descriptions, and graphics.

Course summary

This section provides a text summary of the entire course. It is useful for providing closure at the end of the course. The course summary also indicates the next course in this series, if there is one, and lists additional resources you might find useful as you continue to learn about the software.

Glossary

The glossary provides definitions for all of the key terms used in this course.

Index

The index at the end of this manual makes it easy for you to find information about a particular software component, feature, or concept.

Manual conventions

We've tried to keep the number of elements and the types of formatting to a minimum in the manuals. This aids in clarity and makes the manuals more classically elegant looking. But there are some conventions and icons you should know about.

Convention	Description
Italic text	In conceptual text, indicates a new term or feature.
Bold text	In unit summaries, indicates a key term or concept. In an independent practice activity, indicates an explicit item that you select, choose, or type.
`Code font`	Indicates code or syntax.
`Longer strings of ▶ code will look ▶ like this.`	In the hands-on activities, any code that's too long to fit on a single line is divided into segments by one or more continuation characters (▶). This code should be entered as a continuous string of text.
Select **bold item**	In the left column of hands-on activities, bold sans-serif text indicates an explicit item that you select, choose, or type.
Keycaps like (↵ ENTER)	Indicate a key on the keyboard you must press.

Hands-on activities

The hands-on activities are the most important parts of our manuals. They are divided into two primary columns. The "Here's how" column gives short instructions to you about what to do. The "Here's why" column provides explanations, graphics, and clarifications. Here's a sample:

Do it!

A-1: Creating a commission formula

Here's how	Here's why
1 Open Sales	This is an oversimplified sales compensation worksheet. It shows sales totals, commissions, and incentives for five sales reps.
2 Observe the contents of cell F4	 $\boxed{\text{F4} \quad \blacktriangledown} \quad \boxed{= \quad =\text{E4*C\_Rate}}$ The commission rate formulas use the name "C_Rate" instead of a value for the commission rate.

For these activities, we have provided a collection of data files designed to help you learn each skill in a real-world business context. As you work through the activities, you will modify and update these files. Of course, you might make a mistake and, therefore, want to re-key the activity starting from scratch. To make it easy to start over, you will rename each data file at the end of the first activity in which the file is modified. Our convention for renaming files is to add the word "My" to the beginning of the file name. In the above activity, for example, a file called "Sales" is being used for the first time. At the end of this activity, you would save the file as "My sales," thus leaving the "Sales" file unchanged. If you make a mistake, you can start over using the original "Sales" file.

In some activities, however, it may not be practical to rename the data file. If you want to retry one of these activities, ask your instructor for a fresh copy of the original data file.

Topic B: Setting your expectations

Properly setting your expectations is essential to your success. This topic will help you do that by providing:

- Prerequisites for this course
- A description of the target student at whom the course is aimed
- A list of the objectives for the course
- A skills assessment for the course

Course prerequisites

Before taking this course, you should be familiar with personal computers and the use of a keyboard and a mouse. Furthermore, this course assumes that you've completed the following courses or have equivalent experience:

- *Windows XP: Basic, Windows Vista: Basic,* or *Windows 7: Basic*
- *Access 2013: Basic, MOS Edition*

Target student

You should be comfortable using a personal computer and Microsoft Windows XP or later. You should also have some experience in using Access 2013. You will get the most out of this course if your goal is to become proficient in using more advanced Access features, such as table relationships, referential integrity, joins, queries, forms, reports, charts, PivotTables, and PivotTable charts and forms.

Course objectives

These overall course objectives will give you an idea about what to expect from the course. It is also possible that they will help you see that this course is not the right one for you. If you think you either lack the prerequisite knowledge or already know most of the subject matter to be covered, you should let your instructor know that you think you are misplaced in the class.

After completing this course, you will know how to:

- Normalize tables, analyze tables, and view object dependencies; set table relationships; implement referential integrity between related tables; and set cascading deletes and updates.
- Create lookup fields and multi-valued fields; modify lookup field properties; and use a subdatasheet to add data to related tables.
- Create join queries; create calculated fields in a query; and use queries to view summarized and grouped data.
- Add unbound controls, graphics, and calculated fields to a form; and create multiple-item forms, split forms, datasheet forms, and subforms.
- Add headers and footers in a report; use functions to add calculated values in a report; print database objects and database documents; and create labels.
- Create and modify charts in forms and reports.

Skills inventory

Use the following form to gauge your skill level entering the class. For each skill listed, rate your familiarity from 1 to 5, with five being the most familiar. *This is not a test.* Rather, it is intended to provide you with an idea of where you're starting from at the beginning of class. If you're wholly unfamiliar with all the skills, you might not be ready for the class. If you think you already understand all of the skills, you might need to move on to the next course in the series. In either case, you should let your instructor know as soon as possible.

Skill	1	2	3	4	5
Converting a table to first, second, and third normal forms					
Establishing one-to-one, one-to-many, and many-to-many table relationships					
Using the Table Analyzer					
Identifying object dependencies					
Planning table relationships					
Working with orphan records					
Setting and testing cascading deletes and cascading updates					
Creating and modifying lookup fields and multi-valued fields					
Changing a text box control to a combo box control					
Entering data in a related table					
Using the Query Wizard and Design view to create joins					
Creating inner and outer joins					
Creating a join with an intermediate table					
Creating self-join queries					
Finding records that do not match between tables					
Creating calculated fields in a query and changing the format of displayed values					
Using the Expression Builder in queries					
Creating a query to display summary values					
Using queries to concatenate values					
Grouping controls on a form and drawing rectangles					

Skill	1	2	3	4	5
Changing the tab order for a form					
Adding graphics to forms, and embedding graphics					
Creating calculated fields on a form, and binding a control to a calculated field					
Aligning controls on a form					
Formatting a form for printing					
Adding a combo box to a form and modifying its properties					
Creating multiple-item forms					
Creating split forms					
Creating datasheet forms					
Creating subforms					
Creating navigation forms					
Adding report headers and report footers					
Applying conditional formatting in reports					
Keeping parts of a report on the same page, and forcing a new page in a report					
Adding controls to group footers in reports					
Arranging data in columns on reports					
Adding a background image					
Working with the DateDiff and IIF functions					
Creating subreports					
Printing database objects and a database document					
Creating labels					
Creating and enhancing a chart in a form					
Adding a chart to a report and modifying the chart					

Topic C: Re-keying the course

If you have the proper hardware and software, you can re-key this course after class. This section explains what you'll need in order to do so, and how to do it.

Hardware requirements

Your personal computer should have:

- A keyboard and a mouse
- Pentium 1 GHz processor (or faster)
- 1 GB RAM (or higher)
- 1.5 GB of available hard drive space
- CD-ROM drive
- A monitor with at least 1024 × 768 resolution

Software requirements

You will also need the following software:

- Microsoft Windows 7
- Microsoft Office 2013 (minimally, you can install only Access)

Network requirements

The following network components and connectivity are also required for re-keying this course:

- Internet access, for the following purposes:
  - Updating the Windows operating system and Microsoft Office 2013

Setup instructions to re-key the course

Before you re-key the course, you will need to set up your computer.

1 Install Windows 7 on an NTFS partition according to the software publisher's instructions. After installation is complete, if your machine has Internet access, use Windows Update to install any critical updates and Service Packs.

   Note: You can also use Windows Vista or Windows XP, but the screen shots in this course were taken in Windows 7, so your screens will look different.

2 With flat-panel displays, we recommend using the panel's native resolution for best results. Color depth/quality should be set to High (24 bit) or higher.

3 Install Microsoft Office 2013 according to the software manufacturer's instructions, as follows:

   a When prompted for the CD key, enter the code included with your software.

   b Select "Customize installation" and click Next.

   c Click the Installation Options tab.

   d For Microsoft Office Access, Office Shared Features, and Office Tools, click the down-arrow and choose "Run all from My Computer."

   e Set all except the following to Not Available: Microsoft Office Access, Office Shared Features, and Office Tools.

   f Click Install Now.

4 Update Microsoft Office 2013 as follows:

   a Open Windows Update. Under "Get updates for other Microsoft products", click "Find out more."

   b Check "I agree to the Terms of Use for Microsoft Update" and click Next.

   c Choose "Use recommended settings" and click Install.

5 If you have the data disc that came with this manual, locate the Student Data folder on it and copy it to your Windows desktop.

   If you don't have the data disc, you can download the Student Data files for the course:

   a Connect to http://downloads.logicaloperations.com.

   b Enter the course title or search by part to locate this course

   c Click the course title to display a list of available downloads.
   Note: Data Files are located under the Instructor Edition of the course.

   d Click the link(s) for downloading the Student Data files.

   e Create a folder named Student Data on the desktop of your computer.

   f Double-click the downloaded zip file(s) and drag the contents into the Student Data folder.

6   Start Microsoft Office Access 2013. Then do the following:

    a   Activate the software and click Finish.

    b   Start Access 2013.

    c   Click Blank desktop database. The Blank desktop database dialog box opens.

    d   Click the browse button and navigate to the Topic A folder in the Unit 1 folder in the Student Data folder.

    e   Give the database a filename of Database1, and click OK.

    f   Click Create to open the database.

    g   On the File tab, click Options. In the Access Options dialog box, click Trust Center and then click Trust Center Settings. In the Trust Center dialog box, click Macro Settings and select Enable All Macros. This will prevent a security warning from appearing every time you open a database file. Click OK twice to close the dialog boxes.

    h   Close Access.

Unit 1

Relational databases

Complete this unit, and you'll know how to:

A Normalize tables, use the Table Analyzer, and identify object dependencies.

B Set relationships between tables, and print a report listing the table relationships.

C Implement referential integrity between related tables.

Topic A: Database normalization

Explanation   The key to creating a well-designed database is to divide the data into the right fields and place the fields in the right tables. Correctly designed tables are called *normalized* or *in normal form*. Normalized tables are low-maintenance because they have little duplicate data, and they are flexible and adaptable, absorbing business changes without extensive redesign.

The rules of normalization

The rules of normalization define normalized tables and help organize data into appropriate tables and fields. Each rule must be satisfied before the next is applied. The rules of normalization can be rather technical and abstract. But you don't need to be an expert in normalization to benefit from the basics. This topic presents the first three rules of normalization.

Normalized tables are defined as being in 1NF, 2NF, or 3NF, depending on whether they comply with the first, second, or third normal form.

Pre-normalization exercise

Before considering the first rule of normalization:

1   Make a list of the fields needed for tables, queries, and reports.
2   Group the fields by topic. Each topic represents a proposed database table.
3   Label each table with a name and a phrase that defines its topic.
4   Mark the field (or fields) that uniquely identify each row. This field will be the table's primary key.

First rule of normalization:
Take small bites and no repeating

Your table complies with the first rule of normalization (1NF) if each field contains the smallest meaningful value and if the table has no repeating groups of fields.

Part 1 of rule 1

To determine if a field contains the smallest meaningful value, decide if you'll want to sort, group by, or print a subset of the information in that field. If so, break it into separate fields.

For example, if you have a single field called Contact Address that contains Street Address, City, Region/State, and Postal Code, break this into four fields.

Should you split the new Street Address field into Street Number, Street Name, and Suite/Apartment Number fields? Usually not, because this information is rarely divided. However, if the database is being developed for a fire department that needs neighborhood reports grouped by street name or by ranges of street numbers, then separate the parts of the street address field.

Part 2 of rule 1

It is better to add rows to tables than to add fields. Why? Because queries are optimized to sort, group, and total in one column at a time, and there is no fixed limit on the number of rows you can have. Adding more fields can be inconvenient and requires that you modify linked queries, forms, and reports.

To determine if a table contains repeating groups of fields, list some sample rows of data. If the same kind of information occurs in more than one field, or if you foresee adding more fields to hold variations of this information, then you have repeating groups of fields.

The remedy is to move them to a separate table and list all of the data in one column.

Some common examples of repeating groups of fields are:

- Budget amounts in columns called Q1, Q2, Q3, Q4 or Jan, Feb, Mar, Apr, etc.
- Numeric responses to survey questions in columns named Answer1, Answer2, Answer3, etc.
- Items assigned or loaned to employees in columns labeled Item1, Item2, etc.

In each case, the databases will require more fields as time goes on. How would you calculate the average value of all responses for a 55-question survey? You'd need to write a formula (Answer1 + Answer2 + Answer3…) to add each of the 55 answers in each row and then take the average of that sum!

However, if we remove the question fields from this table and create a table with a Survey Taker ID column, a Question ID column, and just one Response Value column, and then list the responses in 55 rows instead of 55 columns, we can now group and calculate sums, averages, and maximums with ease for the entire sample, for each survey, or for each question. As you add more questions, just add more records, not more fields.

At this point, all tables have fields with the smallest meaningful data and no repeating groups of fields. Now we can apply the second and third rules of normalization.

Do it!

A-1: Discussing the first normal form

Questions and answers
1 What are the two main requirements of the first normal form? Discuss examples.
2 In a customer database, is it better to store the customer's whole name in one field, or in two or three fields? Why?
3 A sales table has separate fields for first-, second-, third-, and fourth-quarter sales totals. Is this normalized? Why or why not?

Second and third rules of normalization: Don't stray from the topic

Explanation

The second and third rules are very similar. Your table complies with the second and third rules of normalization if each non-key field in the table stores data that is a direct fact about the entire primary-key value.

If a field's data is not a direct fact about the entire primary-key value, then pull that field out of that table and put it in a table where it relates to the whole primary key.

The second rule of normalization

The second rule of normalization (second normalized form, or 2NF) says that each non-key field must relate to the whole *multiple-field* primary key. If your table has a single-field primary key, then skip the second rule and use the third .

In a table with a multiple-field primary key, look at each non-key field and ask: does part of the primary key provide enough information to indicate what the value of the non-key field should be? If so, move the non-key field to another table.

Suppose that customers can participate in more than one discount program. The Customer_ID and Discount_ID make up the primary key in a table that also has non-key fields called Discount_% and Sales_Rep. Consider the Sales_Rep field. In this company, one sales rep works with a customer no matter what discount program that customer uses. So knowing the customer ID is enough to determine who the sales rep is. Consider the Discount_%. If there is a fixed percentage for the program, then it relates to only part of the primary key and should be cut from this table. However, if there can be a different percentage for different customers and programs, then it relates to the whole primary key, and Discount_% belongs in this table.

The third rule of normalization

The third rule of normalization (third normalized form, or 3NF) says that each non-key field must relate to the *single-field* primary key

If your table has a single-field primary key, look at each non-key field and ask if this data is a one-to-one fact about the primary-key value. It is not a one-to-one fact if this non-key field actually correlates better to another field in this table or another table, or if you can have more than one value of this field for each row.

For example, in a table about customers, we have the Customer ID field as the primary key, and we have non-key fields called CustFirstName, CustLastName, 1stOrderDate, and PkgWeight. Consider 1stOrderDate. It is a fact about the customer, and there can be only one original order date for one customer ID, so 1stOrderDate can stay in this table. Consider PkgWeight. It relates more closely to orders than to customers, and there can be more than one PkgWeight associated with one customer ID, so it should be moved to a table about orders.

Steps to normalization

Remember these rules, understand your business, and keep working through these questions until your tables are sufficiently normalized.

First rule: Take small bites and no repeating.

- If you need to sort, group by, or print a subset of the information in the field, break it up.

- Do you see the same kind of information in more than one field? Is it possible that you'll need to add more fields in the future to hold additional variations of this kind of data? If so, move this information to one tall field in another table.

Second rule: Stay on topic! Each non-key field must relate to the entire multiple-field primary key.

- Does the data in part of the multiple-field primary key provide enough information to indicate what the value of the non-key field should be? If so, move that non-key field to another table.

- Does the value in the non-key field correspond directly to the combination of values in the multiple-field primary key? If not, move that non-key field to another table.

Third rule: Stay on topic! Each non-key field must relate to the entire single-field primary key.

- Is the data in this non-key field a fact about the primary key? If not, move that non-key field to another table.

- Could we have more than one non-key field for a single primary-key field? If so, move that non-key field to another table.

Do it!

A-2: Discussing the second and third normal forms

Questions and answers
1 A table can be in second normal form without being in first normal form. True or false?
2 Your sales representatives database contains the company name and company address of each rep you deal with, along with the rep's other information. The company name and address are also kept in the vendor company table. How would you normalize these tables?
3 Discuss some examples of situations when strict adherence to normalization rules might be impractical.

The Table Analyzer

Explanation

The Table Analyzer is a wizard that examines a table's structure. If the wizard detects duplicated data in a table, it suggests splitting the table to create two new tables, each of which will contain data that is stored only once. This process normalizes the table, making the table and its database perform more efficiently.

To use the Table Analyzer:

1 On the Database Tools tab, in the Analyze group, click Analyze Table. The wizard opens.

2 Click Next to display the next page in the wizard. Click Next again.

3 Select the table you want to analyze and click Next.

4 Verify that "Yes, let the wizard decide" is selected, and click Next.

5 Observe the groupings that the wizard has created, and change them if necessary, as shown in Exhibit 1-1.

6 Name the new tables and click Next.

7 If the wizard finds potential typographical errors, either confirm the proposed changes or select "Leave as is" in the Correction column. Click Next.

8 Choose whether or not to create a query, and click Next.

9 Click Finish.

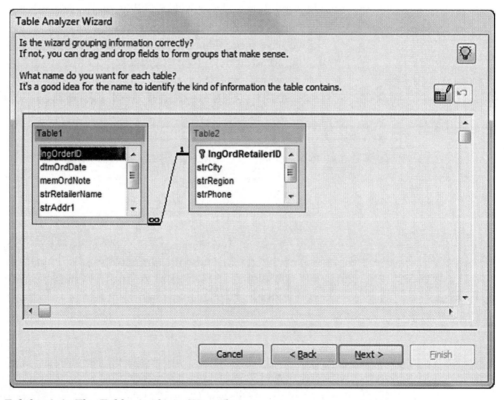

Exhibit 1-1: The Table Analyzer Wizard

Do it!

A-3: Using the Table Analyzer

The files for this activity are in Student Data folder **Unit 1\Topic A**.

Here's how	Here's why
1 Start Microsoft Access 2013	Click Start and choose All Programs, Microsoft Office 2013, Access 2013.
2 Open Orders1	(On the File tab, click Open and browse to the current topic folder.) One of the tables in this database contains repeating information. You'll use the Table Analyzer to normalize it.
3 On the Database Tools tab, click **Analyze Table**	(In the Analyze group.) The Table Analyzer Wizard appears and displays the Looking At the Problem page.
Click **Next**	The wizard displays the Solving the Problem page.
Click **Next**	The table selection page appears.
4 Select **tblOrder**	If necessary.
Click **Next**	The wizard prompts you to decide which fields go in what tables.
5 Verify that **Yes, let the wizard decide** is selected	◉ Yes, let the wizard decide.
Click **Next**	The wizard creates two new tables from the original.
6 Observe the grouping of the fields	StrRetailerName, strAddr1, and strPostalCode are included in Table1. It would be better if they were in Table2 with the rest of the retailer information.
7 Drag **strRetailerName** to just below lngOrdRetailerID in Table 2, as shown	Table2 ⚷ **lngOrdRetailerID** strRetailerName strCity strRegion strPhone lngRep To group this field more logically.
Drag **strAddr1** to just below strRetailerName	

8	Drag **strPostalCode** to just below strRegion	
9	Click [icon]	(The Rename Table button is on the right side of the wizard.) The Table Analyzer Wizard dialog box appears. You'll rename Table2.
	Edit the table name to read **tblRetailers**	
	Click **OK**	To close the dialog box and rename the table.
10	Change the name of Table1 to **tblOrders**	Click Table1 to select it; then click the Rename Table button. Edit the table name and click OK.
11	Click **Next**	The wizard asks if the bold fields uniquely identify each record. They are the ID fields.
	Under tblOrders, select **lngOrderID**	
	Click [key icon]	To make lngOrderID the primary key for tblOrders.
	Click **Next**	The final page of the wizard appears. The wizard prompts you to create a query.
12	Select **No, don't create the query**	The query will not be created.
	Click **Finish**	To close the wizard and create the two new tables.
13	Observe the Navigation Pane	The two new tables you created are listed with the original tables.
14	Observe the open tables	The tblOrders and tblRetailers tables are open.
	Observe tblRetailers	This new table holds the retailer information.
	Observe tblOrders	This new table holds the order information and includes a lookup field for the retailer.
15	On the File tab, click **Close**	

Object dependencies

Explanation

A database object depends on other objects for source data and serves as a source to other objects. As a database becomes more complex, so do its dependencies. Before you delete or modify a database object, such as a table, query, form, or report, it's best to examine that object's relationship to other objects.

The Object Dependencies pane displays those objects that depend on—and are depended on by—the selected object. To examine dependencies, click Object Dependencies on the Database Tools tab.

Before you can use the Object Dependencies feature, the "Track name AutoCorrect info" option must be checked in the Current Database category in the Access Options dialog box. This feature is enabled by default when you create a new database. If it is disabled when you click Object Dependencies, Access 2013 prompts you to enable the feature from within a dialog box.

Once the Object Dependencies pane is open, you can click the plus (+) sign beside any object to view its dependencies, up to four levels. This pane can show both objects that depend on the selected object, and objects that the selected object depends on.

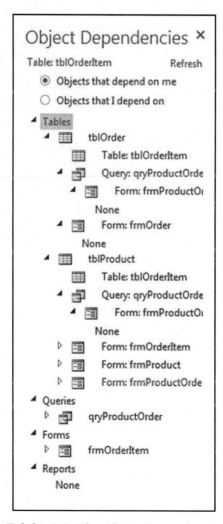

Exhibit 1-2: The Object Dependencies pane

Do it!

A-4:   Identifying object dependencies

The files for this activity are in Student Data folder **Unit 1\Topic A**.

Here's how	Here's why
1 Open Transactions1	(From the current topic folder.) You'll examine the dependencies for a table.
2 In the Navigation Pane, select **tblOrderItem**	
3 On the Database Tools tab, click **Object Dependencies**	You are prompted to enable the "Track name AutoCorrect info" option.
Click **OK**	To enable the Track name AutoCorrect info option. The Object Dependencies pane appears on the right side of the Access window.
Expand the Object Dependencies pane	Point to the left border and drag to the left.
4 Observe the dependencies	The pane shows that two tables, a query, and a form depend on tblOrderItem.
5 Click the arrow beside **tblOrder**	To see the objects that depend on that table. The tree shows that tblOrderItem, qryProductOrder, and frmOrder all depend on tblOrder.
6 At the top of the pane, select **Objects that I depend on**	To see the objects that tblOrderItem depends on: tblOrder and tblProduct.
Close the Object Dependencies pane	
7 Close the database	

Topic B: Table relationships

This topic covers the following Microsoft Office Specialist exam objectives for Access 2013.

#	Objective
1.2	**Manage Relationships and Keys**
1.2.2	Create and modify relationships
1.2.4	Enforce referential integrity
1.2.5	Set foreign keys
1.2.6	View relationships

Defining table relationships

Explanation

Tables in a database can be connected to each other through relationships. You use relationships to extract data from several tables at the same time. For example, to get information about each employee's pay record, you need to create a relationship between the Employees table and the Employee Payroll table.

You can create three types of relationships between tables:

- One-to-one
- One-to-many
- Many-to-many

Although you can link many tables together, you create the relationships between just two tables at a time: a primary table and the related table. The primary and related tables are determined based on the logical relationship between them. The tables are related based on a matching field, which is the primary key of the primary table. When the primary key of one table exists in the related table, the key in the related table is called the *foreign key*.

The one-to-one relationship

Two tables have a *one-to-one* relationship when one complete record in the primary table is related to only one record in the related table, and vice versa, as shown in Exhibit 1-4. For example, each employee record in the Employees table has only one corresponding record in the EmployeeHR table, and vice versa. Usually, the data in the related table is dependent on the data in the primary table, but in a one-to-one relationship, both tables are equally dependent on each other.

Join types

A *join* is an association that specifies how data between tables is related. When you create a relationship between two tables, you can use the Join Properties dialog box, shown in Exhibit 1-3, to set the default join type for the tables. By setting the join type, you control the type of join used by default when you are creating queries based on the related tables. You can change this default when you create a query. This setting has no effect on the relationship itself, and you don't need to set it when you create a relationship.

The Join Properties dialog box provides the following three types of joins:

Option	Join type	Description
1	Inner	Includes all records for which the first table has an exact match in the second table. This is the default join type.
2	Outer (Left)	Includes all records from one table, and only those records from the second table that have a match in the first.
3	Outer (Right)	Includes all records from the second table, and only those records in the first table that have a match in the second.

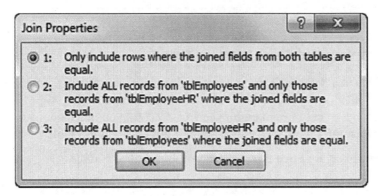

Exhibit 1-3: The Join Properties dialog box

To establish a table relationship:

1. On the Database Tools tab, click the Relationships button to open the Relationships window.
2. On the Relationship Tools | Design tab, click Show Table to open the Show Table dialog box.
3. Select the desired table and click Add to add the table to the Relationships window. Add as many tables as necessary. You can also drag tables from the Navigation Pane to the Relationships window.
4. Click Close to close the Show Table dialog box.
5. In the Relationships window, drag the desired field from the first table to the desired field in the second table. The Edit Relationships dialog box appears.
6. (Optional) Click Join Type to open the Join Properties dialog box if you want to change the default join type for queries. Click OK to close the dialog box.
7. Check Enforce Referential Integrity and click Create.

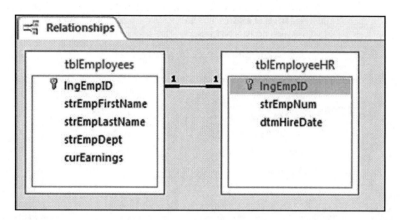

Exhibit 1-4: The Relationships window, showing a one-to-one relationship

Do it!

B-1:   Establishing a one-to-one table relationship

The files for this activity are in Student Data folder **Unit 1\Topic B**.

Here's how	Here's why
1 Open Employees2	From the current topic folder.
2 On the Database Tools tab, click **Relationships**	(In the Relationships group.) To open the Relationships window. The Relationship Tools | Design tab appears on the Ribbon.
3 On the Design tab, click **Show Table**	(In the Relationships group.) To open the Show Table dialog box. It contains tabs for various database objects.
4 Verify that the Tables tab is active	It lists all of the tables in the database.
5 From the list of tables, select **tblEmployees**	
6 Click **Add**	To add the table to the Relationships window.
7 Add **tblEmployeeHR** to the Relationships window	Select tblEmployeeHR from the list and click Add.
8 Click **Close**	To close the Show Table dialog box.
Observe the Relationships window	It lists the fields for both tables.

9	Drag the **lngEmpID** field from tblEmployees to lngEmpID in tblEmployeeHR, as shown	

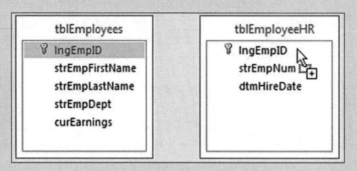

	(The pointer changes to a field symbol while you're dragging.) The Edit Relationships dialog box appears as soon as you drop the field.
10 Click **Join Type**	To open the Join Properties dialog box. It controls the type of join to be used by default when you're creating queries based on the related tables. This setting has no effect on the relationship itself, and you don't need to set it when you create a relationship.
11 Click **OK**	To close the Join Properties dialog box without changing the default.
12 Check **Enforce Referential Integrity**	To ensure that data in the related tables match.
13 Click **Create**	To create the relationship.
Observe the Relationships window	As shown in Exhibit 1-4. A line appears between the tblEmployees and tblEmployeeHR tables. The number 1 appears on both sides of the line. This means that the tables have a one-to-one relationship.
14 Click 🖫	(On the Quick Access toolbar.) To update the relationship.

The one-to-many relationship

Explanation

Two tables have a *one-to-many* relationship when one record in the primary table has several corresponding records in the related table, while a record in the related table has only one corresponding record in the primary table.

For example, in the tblEmployee and tblDept tables, an employee can belong to only one department, but a department can contain many employees. Here, tblDept is the primary table and tblEmployee is the related table.

Do it!

B-2:   Establishing a one-to-many table relationship

Here's how	Here's why
1 Open the Show Table dialog box	Click the Show Table button on the Relationship Tools | Design tab.
2 Add **tblDept** and **tblEmployee** to the Relationships window	(Select each table from the list and click Add.) You'll create a relationship between these tables. Arrange the tables as necessary.
Close the Show Table dialog box	
3 Drag **strDeptCode** from tblDept to **strEmpDept** in tblEmployee	The Edit Relationships dialog box appears.
4 Check **Enforce Referential Integrity**	
5 Click **Create**	To create the relationship.
Observe the relationship between tblDept and tblEmployee	A line connects tblDept and tblEmployee. The number 1 appears on the tblDept side of the line, and an infinity sign (∞) appears on the tblEmployee side. This means that the tables have a one-to-many relationship.

6 Update the relationship

7 Close the Relationships window

Close the database

The many-to-many relationship

Explanation
Two tables have a *many-to-many* relationship when several records in one table are related to several records in another table. For example, in an Order Entry database, an order can contain several products, and the same product can be present in several orders. Hence, the tblOrder and tblProduct tables will have a many-to-many relationship.

Using a junction table

A *junction table* is used to create a many-to-many relationship between two tables. A junction table is needed because you can't create a many-to-many relationship directly in Access 2013. Consider the relationship between tblProducts and tblOrder. The primary keys—Product ID in the tblProduct table, and Order ID in the tblOrder table—aren't directly related to each other.

To relate such tables, you first create a junction table that contains the primary keys of both of the tables. For example, the tblOrderItem table, containing the Order ID and Product ID, can be the junction table between tblProduct and tblOrder, as shown in Exhibit 1-5. Creating a one-to-many relationship between tblProduct and tblOrderItem, and between tblOrder and tblOrderItem, creates a many-to-many relationship between tblProduct and tblOrder.

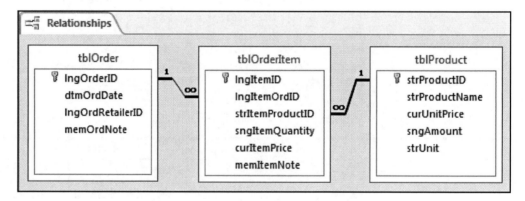

Exhibit 1-5: A many-to-many relationship, using a junction table

Do it!   **B-3:   Establishing a many-to-many table relationship**

The files for this activity are in Student Data folder Unit 1\Topic B.

Here's how	Here's why
1 Open Orders2	From the current topic folder.
2 On the Database Tools tab, click **Relationships**	To open the Relationships window. The Relationship Tools | Design tab appears.
3 Add **tblOrder**, **tblOrderItem**, and **tblProduct** to the Relationships window	You'll create relationships between these tables. (Click Show Table. Close the Show Table dialog box when you're done.)
4 Drag **lngOrderID** from tblOrder to **lngItemOrdID** in tblOrderItem	The Edit Relationships dialog box appears.
5 Check **Enforce Referential Integrity**	To ensure that the fields in the related tables match.
Click **Create**	To create the relationship.
6 Create a one-to-many relationship between the tblProduct and tblOrderItem tables	Use the Product ID field as the join field to create the relationship. Drag strProductID from tblProduct to strItemProductID in tblOrderItem.
Observe the relationships between tblOrder, tblOrderItem, and tblProduct	(The Relationships window should look like Exhibit 1-5.) A line appears between tblOrder and tblOrderItem, showing a one-to-many relationship between these tables. A similar relationship exists between tblProduct and tblOrderItem. The tblProduct and tblOrder tables have a many-to-many relationship that is defined by both tables having a one-to-many relationship with tblOrderItem, which is the junction table.
7 Update the relationship and close the database	

Topic C: Referential integrity

This topic covers the following Microsoft Office Specialist exam objectives for Access 2013.

#	Objective
1.2	**Manage Relationships and Keys**
1.2.4	Enforce referential integrity
1.2.6	View Relationships

Requirements for referential integrity

Explanation

A database has *referential integrity* when all values in a related table have corresponding values in the primary table. Without referential integrity, for instance, removing a product from the Products table might leave unrelated records in the Orders table. When referential integrity is implemented, changes or deletions in records are reflected throughout related tables. In addition, if you attempt to implement referential integrity while creating a new relationship, there can be no unrelated records. If there are, an error is generated, and the relationship is not created.

The following conditions must be met for referential integrity to be implemented:

- The primary table has a primary key.
- The related fields have the same data type.
- The tables belong to the same database.

The Cascading Update and Cascading Delete options preserve the referential integrity between tables by ensuring that any changes in the primary table are reflected in the related tables.

Planning relationships between tables

You should always plan and set relationships between tables to ensure referential integrity. Implementing referential integrity between related tables prevents you from making changes in the primary table that result in unrelated records in a related table. For example, in the tblProduct table, you can't delete a Product ID that has corresponding orders in the tblOrderItem table.

To edit an existing relationship, double-click the line between the tables in the Relationships window to open the Edit Relationships dialog box.

Do it!

C-1: Planning table relationships

The files for this activity are in Student Data folder **Unit 1\Topic C**.

Here's how	Here's why
1 Open Orders3	From the current topic folder.
2 Open tblProduct	(Double-click it in the Navigation Pane.) To view the contents of this table.
3 Open tblOrderItem	A new tab appears for the table. You switch between tables by clicking the tabs.
4 In the tblOrderItem table, observe the Order Detail ID and Product columns	The Product column for Order Detail IDs 2 and 14 contains P0003. The same product can be present in several orders.
In the tblProduct table, observe the Product ID column	There is a one-to-many relationship between the tblProduct and tblOrderItem tables, with Product ID as the linking field. Enforcing referential integrity between these tables ensures that if product P0003 is deleted from tblProduct, all orders including product P0003 will be deleted from tblOrderItem.
5 In the tblProduct table, delete record 3	(Select the record and press Delete.) A message box warns you that the record cannot be deleted.
Click **OK**	
6 Close tblOrderItem and tblProduct	

Orphan records

Explanation

If you set a relationship between two tables, every record in the related table must have a corresponding record in the primary table. To ensure that this occurs, you can enable referential integrity between the tables. If data is modified or deleted in the primary table, the related table should also be updated. For example, if you remove a product from the tblProduct table, you should also remove all orders including that product from the tblOrderItem table.

Deleting a product from the tblProduct table without deleting the related records in the tblOrderItem table will result in *orphan records*—records with no related record in a primary table. Such records can get lost and take up disk space without being of any use.

Do it!

C-2: Working with orphan records

Here's how	Here's why
1 Open the Relationships window	(Click the Relationships button on the Database Tools tab.) You'll remove referential integrity between tables.
2 Double-click the line between tblOrderItem and tblProduct	To open the Edit Relationships dialog box.
In the Table/Query list, select **tblProduct**	If necessary.
3 Clear **Enforce Referential Integrity**	To remove referential integrity between the tables.
Click **OK**	
Observe the window	The number 1 and the infinity sign between the tables no longer appear, indicating that referential integrity between the tables isn't set.
4 Close the Relationships window	Your changes are saved as you make them.
5 Open tblProduct	The value in the Product ID column of the third record is P0003. You'll delete this record.
6 Delete record 3	(Select record 3, press Delete, and click Yes in the Microsoft Access dialog box.) To delete the record for product P0003. Because referential integrity is not being enforced, Access allows the record to be deleted.
Close tblProduct	
7 Open tblOrderItem	
Observe records 2 and 14	The Product column for these records contains P0003. These records are orphan records because P0003 has been removed from tblProduct. As a result, they are not related to any records in that table.
8 Delete records 2 and 14	
9 Close tblOrderItem	

Cascading deletes

Explanation

You can use *cascading deletes* to remove records in related tables simultaneously, thereby maintaining referential integrity. When you use cascading deletes to delete a record from a primary table, Access automatically deletes all related records from the related tables. This feature ensures that there are no orphan records in the related tables.

To enforce referential integrity with cascading deletes:

1 Open the Relationships window.
2 Double-click the line between the tables for which you want to implement cascading deletes. The Edit Relationships dialog box appears.
3 Check Enforce Referential Integrity.
4 Check Cascade Delete Related Records.
5 Click OK to close the Edit Relationships dialog box.

When you use cascading deletes, all related records in related tables are deleted automatically. For example, if you delete the record of Product ID P0001 from the tblProduct table, all of the records in the tblOrderItem table containing Product P0001 are also deleted.

To test cascading deletes:

1 Open the desired table.
2 Navigate to the record that you want to delete.
3 Press the Delete key. A warning message indicates how many records will be deleted in the related tables.
4 Click Yes to delete the record.
5 Update and close the table.
6 Open a related table to confirm that all of the related records have been deleted. Then close the table.

Do it!   ## C-3:   Setting cascading deletes

Here's how	Here's why
1 Open the Relationships window	
2 Double-click the line between tblOrderItem and tblProduct	The Edit Relationships dialog box appears. You'll modify the relationship between these tables.
In the Table/Query list, select **tblProduct**	If necessary.
Observe the dialog box	The options under Enforce Referential Integrity aren't available.
3 Check **Enforce Referential Integrity**	The options are now available.
Check **Cascade Delete Related Records**	To cascade deletes between the tables.
Click **OK**	To modify the relationship and close the dialog box.
4 Close the Relationships window	
5 Open tblOrderItem	There are several records with P0001 in the product field; records 1, 5, 23, 59, and 63.
Close tblOrderItem	
6 Open tblProduct	You'll test cascading deletes by deleting a record from this table.
7 Verify that Product ID P0001 is selected	You'll delete the details of the product with Product ID P0001.
Delete the first record	A message warns you that deleting the current record will cause records to be deleted in related tables.
Click **Yes**	To delete the record.
8 Open tblOrderItem	To view the modified data in this table.
Observe the table	There are no orders for Product P0001; those records have been deleted. The deletion in tblProduct cascaded to the related records in tblOrderItem.
9 Close the tables	

Cascading updates

Explanation You can use *cascading updates* to maintain referential integrity by updating foreign-key values in related tables simultaneously. This means that whenever you change a primary-key value in a table, the change is updated in all of the related tables. For example, if you change a Product ID in the tblProduct table, the Product field in the tblOrderItem table is updated automatically. You can implement referential integrity for cascading updates by checking the Cascade Update Related Records option in the Edit Relationships dialog box.

Do it!

C-4: Using cascading updates

Here's how	Here's why
1 Open the Relationships window	
Double-click the line between tblOrderItem and tblProduct	You'll modify the relationship between these tables.
In the Table/Query list, select **tblProduct**	If necessary.
2 Check **Cascade Update Related Fields**	To cascade updates between the tables.
Click **OK**	
3 Close the Relationships window	
4 Open tblOrderItem	
Observe the Order Detail ID and Product columns	The Product column in the first record contains P0005.
5 Close tblOrderItem	
6 Open tblProduct	You'll test cascading updates by modifying a record in this table.
7 Change the Product ID of product P0005 to **P0001**	In the third record.
Close tblProduct	
8 Open tblOrderItem	
Observe the first record	The Product for this record is now P0001, indicating that the update in tblProduct cascaded to related records in tblOrderItem.
9 Close the database	

Unit summary: Relational databases

Topic A   In this topic, you learned how to **normalize** tables. You learned that normalization is the process of eliminating redundant data by dividing the database into several related tables. You learned about the first, second, and third rules of normalization. Next, you learned how to use the **Table Analyzer** wizard to normalize tables. Finally, you learned how to identify **object dependencies** in a database.

Topic B   In this topic, you learned how to create **relationships** between tables in a database. You learned that the three types of relationships you can create between tables are one-to-one, one-to-many, and many-to-many. You also learned that you use a **junction table** to create a many-to-many relationship. Finally, you learned how to print table relationships.

Topic C   In this topic, you learned how to implement **referential integrity** between related tables to avoid orphan records. You also learned how to set the **Cascade Delete** and **Cascade Update** options so that when you delete or modify a record in one table, the change is also made in all related fields and tables.

Review questions

1 What are the three rules, in order, of data normalization?

2 What are the three types of relationships that can be created between tables?

3 Table relationships are based on matching fields. When the matching field is the _____ key in a table, that table is known as the primary table, while this field is known as the _____ key in the related table.

4 What is the procedure to establish a table relationship?

5 What is the purpose of creating a junction table?

6 What are the three requirements that must be satisfied before referential integrity can be implemented?

7 What is created when you delete a record from the primary table without deleting the related records in a related table?

Independent practice activity

In this activity, you'll create different types of relationships between tables. You'll also enforce and test cascading deletes between the tables.

The files for this activity are in Student Data folder **Unit 1\Unit summary**.

1 Open OrdersIPA.

2 Open the Relationships window.

3 Create a one-to-many relationship between the tblRetailer and tblOrder tables.

4 Create a one-to-many relationship between the tblOrder and tblOrderItem tables. (*Hint:* You need not add the tblOrder table again.)

5 Save the relationships.

6 Compare the Relationships window to Exhibit 1-6.

7 Enforce cascading deletes between the tblOrderItem and tblOrder tables.

8 Update the relationship.

9 Test cascading deletes between the tblOrder and tblOrderItem tables. (*Hint:* Delete an Order ID in tblOrder, and confirm that all records containing that specific Order ID are deleted from tblOrderItem.)

10 Close the database.

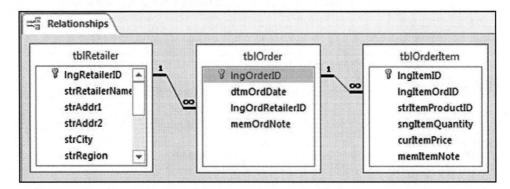

Exhibit 1-6: After Step 5, the Relationships window should look like this

Unit 2

Related tables

Complete this unit, and you'll know how to:

A Use the Lookup Wizard to create a lookup field and a multi-valued field.

B Modify properties for a lookup field.

C Use a subdatasheet to add data to related tables.

Topic A: Creating lookup fields

Explanation

A *lookup field* can contain values from another field in the same or a different table or from a user-defined list. Rather than typing in data, you select the desired value from the drop-down list provided in the lookup field. The list that a lookup field displays is called a *lookup column*. The Lookup Wizard can help you create a lookup field, which you can later modify.

Lookup fields can make data entry easier and ensure that the data entered is valid. For instance, the Product field in an Invoice table could list only the values of the Product Name column in the Product table. This would save typing and ensure that only valid products would be placed in the Invoice table. A lookup field can also display a list of user-defined values, instead of a column from a table or query.

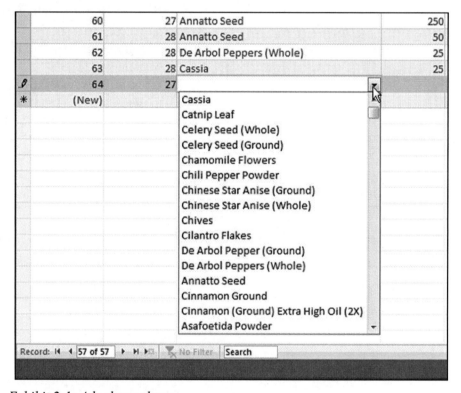

Exhibit 2-1: A lookup column

Looking up values in a table or query

You can create a lookup field in a table's Design view. The lookup field extracts a list of values from another table. Before creating a lookup field, you need to delete any relationships between the tables. This step is required because you cannot change the data type of a field if the table is related to another table.

To create a lookup field that looks up values in a table or query:

1   Delete any relationship between the table where you want to create a lookup field and the table containing the lookup data.

2   Open the table, in Design view, in which you want to create the lookup field.

3   Click in the Data Type column of the field in which you want to create the list. A drop-down arrow appears.

4   Click the drop-down arrow and select Lookup Wizard to start the wizard.

5   Select the first option to specify that you want to look up the values in a table or a query. Click Next.

6   Under View, select the desired option.

7   From the list, select an object. Click Next.

8   From the Available Fields list, select the desired field. Click Add to add the field to the Selected Fields list. Click Next.

9   Select a field based on how the list should be sorted, and click Next. The wizard displays a column of values for the specified field.

10   Widen the column to fit all values in it, if necessary. Click Next.

11   Enter a label for the lookup field, and click Finish. A message box prompts you to save the table.

12   Click Yes to save the table and create the lookup column in the field.

13   Set the relationships between the related fields.

Do it!

A-1:   Creating a lookup field

The files for this activity are in Student Data folder **Unit 2\Topic A**.

Here's how	Here's why
1 Open Products1	From the current topic folder.
2 Open tblOrderItem	The Product column contains the Product IDs for the company's products. The details about each product are stored in the tblProduct table. You want to be able to select a product name from a lookup column, instead of typing the product ID, so you'll make the Product column a lookup field.
3 Switch to Design view	Click the Design View button on the Ribbon or in the status bar.
Click in the Data Type column of strItemProductID	You'll make this field a lookup field.
From the Data Type list, select **Lookup Wizard...**	A warning message states that you cannot change the data type because the field is a part of one or more relationships.
Click **OK**	To close the message box.
4 Close tblOrderItem	A message box asks if you want to save changes in the table design.
Click **No**	To close the table without saving any changes.
5 Open the Relationships window	

6	Delete the relationship between tblOrderItem and tblProduct	In the Relationships window, select the relationship between tblOrderItem and tblProduct, and press Delete. A message box prompts you to confirm the deletion.
	Click **Yes**	To confirm the deletion of the relationship between the two tables.
	Close the Relationships window	
7	Open tblOrderItem in Design view	
	Select the Data Type column of strItemProductID	You'll change the data type of the field.
	From the Data Type list, select **Lookup Wizard...**	To start the Lookup Wizard.
	Verify that the first option is selected	You'll create a lookup column based on field values in a table.
	Click **Next**	
8	Under View, verify that **Tables** is selected	
	From the list, select **Table: tblProduct**	
	Click **Next**	This wizard page shows a list of fields in the table you selected. Here, you can specify the fields on which to base the lookup field.
9	In the Available Fields list, select **strProductName**	You'll create a lookup field based on this field.
	Click ⟩	To add strProductName to the Selected Fields list.
	Click **Next**	The wizard displays options for sorting the list.
	Click **Next**	The list of products appears in the Product Name column. You can resize the column.
	Click **Next**	You'll use strItemProductID as the label.
10	Click **Finish**	A message box prompts you to save the table.
	Click **Yes**	To save the table and create the lookup field.
	Close the table	
11	Open the Relationships window	

12	Create a one-to-many relationship between tblOrderItem and tblProduct	Double-click the relationship line to open the Edit Relationships dialog box.
	Check the indicated options	☑ Enforce Referential Integrity ☑ Cascade Update Related Fields ☑ Cascade Delete Related Records
	Click **OK**	To create the relationship.
13	Update the relationships and close the Relationships window	
14	Open tblOrderItem	
	Observe the Product column	It contains product names instead of Product IDs.
	Expand the column	To fit the product names.
15	Add a new record	There are New Record buttons on the Data tab and at the bottom of the table.
	Press (TAB)	To move to the Order ID cell. (Order Detail ID is an AutoNumber field, so the value will be assigned automatically.)
	Enter **27**	To specify the Order ID.
16	Press (TAB)	To move to the Product cell. A list appears in the cell.
	Click the list arrow	To display the list of product names that were obtained from the tblProduct table, as shown in Exhibit 2-1.
	From the list, select **Chives**	To specify the product name.
17	Press (TAB)	To move to the Quantity cell.
	Enter **170**	
18	Press (TAB)	To move to the Price Paid cell.
	Enter **1.25**	
	Press (TAB)	To move to the Notes cell. The value you entered in the Price Paid column now appears with currency formatting.
19	Update and close the table	

Multi-valued lookup fields

Explanation

You can store more than one value in a field by creating a lookup column that supports multiple values. This can be useful when a field needs to be assigned more than one value. For example, a field that records the source of a spice might require multiple values if the spice is available from more than one region, as shown in Exhibit 2-2.

Microsoft Windows SharePoint began supporting multi-valued fields with Windows SharePoint Services Version 3.0 (an extension of SharePoint Server 2007). If an Access database is exported to a SharePoint list, any multi-valued fields in the Access database are interpreted by SharePoint as one of its multi-valued data types.

You can use multiple values for lookup columns that reference another table, or lookup columns in which you create the list of values. Here's how to create a multi-valued field using a list that you create yourself:

1 In Design view, click the Data Type column and select Lookup Wizard to start the wizard.

2 Select the second option to specify that you want to type the values. Click Next.

3 In Column 1, enter the list of values to be displayed in the list. Click Next.

4 Enter a label for the lookup field.

5 Check Allow Multiple Values and then click Finish.

Exhibit 2-2: A lookup column that supports multiple values

Upsizing to SQL Server

If you need to convert your Access database to a Microsoft SQL Server database at some time in the future, be aware that SQL Server does not support the multi-valued data type. If you migrate an Access database to SQL Server by using SQL Server's Import and Export Wizard, multi-valued fields are converted to long text fields, and the conversion may require manual programming to complete.

Do it!

A-2: Creating a multi-valued lookup field

Here's how	Here's why
1 Open tblProduct in Design view	You'll create a lookup column that supports multiple values.
2 Add a field named **strSource**	
In the Data Type field, select **Lookup Wizard...**	You'll create a lookup field.
Select **I will type in the values that I want.**	
Click **Next**	The wizard displays a blank list.
3 In the first row, type **Africa/Middle East**	To enter the first region.
Enter other regions as shown	

Click **Next**	The final page of the wizard appears.
4 Check **Allow Multiple Values**	To make this lookup column a multi-valued field.
Click **Finish**	To close the wizard.
5 In the Caption field, enter **Source(s)**	In the General properties.
Update the table	To save the changes made in Design view.
6 Switch to Datasheet view	
7 Widen the **Source(s)** field	To about twice its current width. This will make it easier to read the values list.
Click the **Source(s)** field for Cassia	An arrow appears in the cell.
Click the arrow	To display the list.

8	Check both **Americas** and **Asia/Pacific**	As shown in Exhibit 2-2. Cassia is grown in both Asia and South America.
	Click **OK**	To record the selections and close the list.
9	Observe the field	Both values appear, separated by a comma.
10	Update and close the table	
11	Close the database	

Topic B: Modifying lookup fields

Explanation
You can change the appearance of a lookup field by modifying properties such as List Width. You can specify the type of control used by a lookup field to display data. You can also define a fixed set of values, in the form of a value list, for the lookup field.

Setting the Column Heads property will display headings along with the values in a lookup column. If the values in the lookup field are drawn from a table field, then that field's name or caption is used as the heading. The List Width property determines the size of a lookup column. The List Rows property sets the maximum number of values to be displayed in a lookup column.

To display column headings in a lookup column:
1 Open the table in Design view.
2 Under Field Name, click the desired field name.
3 Under Field Properties, click the Lookup tab.
4 From the Column Heads list, select Yes.

Do it!

B-1: Modifying lookup field properties

The files for this activity are in Student Data folder **Unit 2\Topic B**.

Here's how	Here's why
1 Open Products2	
2 Open tblOrderItem	You'll change the lookup column in this table.
Display the lookup column for the Product column	(Click inside the Product column and then click the drop-down arrow.) The list has no heading describing the values in it. Several values in the list are not completely visible.
3 Switch to Design view	You'll display a heading for the values in the list.
4 Display the lookup properties for the strItemProductID field	Click inside the Data Type column of the strItemProductID field. Then, under Field Properties, click the Lookup tab.
5 Click in the Column Heads box	A drop-down arrow appears.
6 Click the drop-down arrow	To display a list.
From the list, select **Yes**	To display column headings along with values in the lookup column. The Property Update Options button appears.
Click as shown	Column Count 2 / Column Heads Yes / Column Widths 0"1" / List Rows 24
	To display a list of options.

7	Observe the options	These are additional options for updating properties.
	Press (ESC)	To close the list.
8	In the lookup properties, edit the List Width box to read **3**	(Do not edit the Column Width box.) To increase the width of the list. The double quote indicates that the value will be in inches.
	Update the table	
	Switch to Datasheet view	
9	Display the lookup column for the Product column of the first record	
	Observe the list	The column heading appears, and all of the values in the list are now completely visible. The lookup column is wider than the field column.
10	Close tblOrderItem	

Changing a lookup field

Explanation

You can change an existing field into a lookup field by using the Lookup tab in the Design view of a table. A field can have the following types of controls:

- **Text box** — Used to enter data in a table. By default, a cell in a table is a text box control.
- **Combo box** — Displays a list of values. You can either select a value from the list or enter a value in the control in the same way that you'd enter values in a text box. You can create a combo box by defining the values in the list manually or by creating a lookup column.
- **List box** — Displays a list of values. With a list box, you can only select a value from the list; you cannot enter a new value.

As with lookup fields created with the Lookup Wizard, a combo box or a list box can use values from a field in a table, or you can enter a list of values.

To change a text box into a combo box control with a fixed list:

1 Open the table in Design view.
2 Under Field Name, click the name of the desired field.
3 Under Field Properties, click the Lookup tab.
4 From the Display Control list, select Combo Box.
5 From the Row Source Type list, select Value List.
6 In the Row Source box, enter the values for the list, with each value separated by a semicolon.

Do it!

B-2:   Changing a text box to a combo box

Here's how	Here's why
1 Open tblProduct in Design view	
2 Under Field Name, click **sngAmount**	
Under Field Properties, click the **Lookup** tab	You'll change the field's properties.
3 From the Display Control list, select **Combo Box**	You'll use a combo box control instead of a text box control. More property boxes appear on the Lookup tab below the Display Control list.
4 From the Row Source Type list, select **Value List**	You'll use a list to enter data in this column. The Property Update Options button appears.
5 Click in the Row Source box	You'll enter values for the value list.
Enter the indicated values	`1; 2; 3; 4; 5; 6` A semicolon and a space separate the values in the list. The spaces make the list easier to read in this field on the Lookup tab; they do not appear in the value list.
6 Update the table	The spaces between values are removed.
7 Switch to Datasheet view	
Click inside the Amount column of the first record	A drop-down arrow appears in the cell.
Click the drop-down arrow	To display a list of values that you can use in this field. The list contains previously specified values.
8 From the list, select **3**	To change the product's unit size.
9 Edit the value to read **3.25**	Because this is a combo box, you can enter values that are not on the list.
10 Close the database	

Topic C: Subdatasheets

Explanation

In Access, you can enter data in related tables simultaneously by using a subdatasheet. A *subdatasheet* is a datasheet within another datasheet. It displays a set of records from a related table, as shown in Exhibit 2-3.

tblProduct				
Product I ▾	Product Name ▾	Unit Price ▾	Amount ▾	Unit
⊞ P0001	Cassia	$3.00	2	oz
⊞ P0002	Catnip Leaf	$2.75	2.25	oz
⊞ P0003	Celery Seed (Whole)	$1.75	1	oz
⊞ P0004	Celery Seed (Ground)	$1.50	1	oz
⊞ P0005	Chamomile Flowers	$1.00	2	oz
⊞ P0006	Chili Pepper Powder	$2.00	2.25	oz
⊞ P0007	Chinese Star Anise (Ground)	$3.50	0.5	oz
⊞ P0008	Chinese Star Anise (Whole)	$1.00	0.5	oz
⊟ P0009	Chives	$1.25	3	oz

Order Detail ▾	Order ID ▾	Quantity ▾	Price Paid ▾	Notes
10	11	170	$1.25	
41	19	100	$1.25	
66	27	170	$1.25	
67	5	100	$1.25	
*	(New)			

⊞ P0010	Cilantro Flakes	$2.00	2.75	oz

Exhibit 2-3: A subdatasheet

The subdatasheet in Exhibit 2-3 displays records from the tblOrderItem table that are related to Product ID P0009. You can use the expand indicator (+) to display the subdatasheet for each record. To close a subdatasheet, you can use the collapse indicator (−).

Using a subdatasheet to add data

You use a subdatasheet to view and enter data in related tables. For example, you can enter orders for a product by inserting the tblOrderItem table as a subdatasheet in the tblProduct table. By default, Access automatically inserts a subdatasheet in a table that has a related table. This subdatasheet will display the related records in the related table. You can also modify the table to display another table as a subdatasheet.

To insert a table as a subdatasheet:

1　Open a table in Design view.

2　On the Table Tools | Design tab, click Property Sheet to open the properties for the table.

3　In the Property Sheet, display the Subdatasheet Name list and select the name of the table that you want to insert as a subdatasheet.

4　Close the Property Sheet and update the table.

Do it!

C-1:　Using a subdatasheet

The files for this activity are in Student Data folder **Unit 2\Topic C**.

Here's how	Here's why
1　Open Products3	
2　Open tblProduct in Design view	
3　In the Show/Hide group on the Design tab, click **Property Sheet**	(If necessary.) To display the properties for the table.
4　From the Subdatasheet Name list, select **Table.tblOrderItem**	Subdatasheet Name Table.tblOrderItem ⯆ (In the Property Sheet.) To add this table as a subdatasheet.
5　Close the Property Sheet 　Update the table	
6　Switch to Datasheet view	A plus sign (+), called an *expand indicator*, now appears to the left of each record. Click it to display the subdatasheet.
7　Navigate to the record of product P0009	(Click inside the Product ID field with the value P0009.) You'll add a record, containing the product Chives, in the tblOrderItem table.
Click the expand indicator to the left of the record	To open the subdatasheet for this record. The expand indicator (+) is replaced by a collapse indicator (–). The records in tblOrderItem containing the product Chives appear.
Place the insertion point within the first row of the subdatasheet	If necessary.

8 Right-click the row header and choose **New Record**

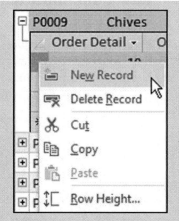

To insert a new record in this related table.

Press [TAB]

To move to the next field. The Order Detail ID field is an AutoNumber field, so a new Order Detail ID is entered automatically.

9 Enter **5**, **100**, and **1.25** in the next three fields, respectively

(These are the fields Order ID, Quantity, and Price Paid.) To add the Chives to Order 5.

10 Click the collapse indicator to the left of the record in tblProduct

To close the subdatasheet.

11 Close the table

12 Open tblOrderItem

To view the new record in the table.

Observe record 67

This is the record you added from the tblProduct table. Notice that the Order ID is 5.

13 Close the database

Unit summary: Related tables

Topic A   In this topic, you learned that a **lookup field** lists data from a field in the same table or another table or a query, or from a user-defined list. You learned that a **multi-valued** field can be assigned one or more values from a lookup column. You also learned how to create lookup fields in a table.

Topic B   In this topic, you learned how to modify **lookup field properties**, such as Column Heads and List Width. You also learned how to change a text box control to a **combo box** control.

Topic C   In this topic, you learned that a **subdatasheet** is used to enter data in related tables. You also learned how to insert a subdatasheet in a table.

Review questions

1 What are the advantages of using lookup fields?

2 Which of the following can be displayed in a lookup field?

A User-defined values

B Values from a table

C Values from a query

D All of the above

3 What must you do before creating a lookup field? Why?

4 What is the difference between a combo box control and a list box control?

5 How do you open the subdatasheet for a record?

Independent practice activity

In this activity, you'll create lookup columns and modify their properties. Then you'll create a subdatasheet and use it to add records to a table.

The files for this activity are in Student Data folder **Unit 2\Unit summary**.

1 Open ProductsIPA.

2 In the tblOrder table, create a lookup column for the field containing the Retailer ID values by using the Retailer Name field from the tblRetailer table. (*Hint:* Delete the relationship between tblOrder and tblRetailer before creating the lookup field.)

3 Create a one-to-many relationship between tblRetailer and tblOrder.

4 Open tblOrder and verify that the Retailer field displays retailer names instead of retailer IDs.

5 In the tblOrderItem table, create a lookup column for the Product ID field to display product names from the tblProduct table.

6 Open tblOrderItem and verify that the Product field displays the product names.

7 Set the List Width property of the lookup column in the Product column of tblOrderItem to 3.

8 Use the Column Heads property to display column headings in the lookup column in tblOrderItem. Then update the table.

9 Display the lookup column for Product in the first record of the tblOrderItem table and compare it to Exhibit 2-4.

10 Add a record to the tblOrderItem table by using the lookup column to enter the product name. Add the product Annatto Seed to the order with Order ID 4. The quantity of the product should be 25, and the price paid should be $1.23.

11 Close the table.

12 Insert the tblOrderItem table as a subdatasheet in the tblProduct table.

13 Add a record to the tblOrderItem table for Product P0005 by using the subdatasheet in the tblProduct table. The Order ID should be 1, the quantity should be 200, and the price paid should be $1.00.

14 Update and close the table.

15 In the tblOrderItem table, view the record that you entered in Step 13.

16 Close the table.

17 Close the database.

Order Detail	Order ID	Product	Quantity	Price Paid
1	1	Cassia	100	$3.00
2	2	Product Name		
3	3	Cassia		
4	4	Catnip Leaf		
5	5	Celery Seed (Whole)		
6	6	Celery Seed (Ground)		
7	7	Chamomile Flowers		
8	9	Chili Pepper Powder		
9	10	Chinese Star Anise (Ground)		
10	11	Chinese Star Anise (Whole)		
11	1	Chives		
12	2	Cilantro Flakes		
13	1	De Arbol Pepper (Ground)		
14	4	De Arbol Peppers (Whole)		
15	4	Annatto Seed		
16	4	Cinnamon Ground		
		Cinnamon (Ground) Extra High Oil (2X)		
17	5	Annatto Seed	25	$1.23
18	6	Cinnamon Grou	4	$14.89
19	7	Asafoetida Pov	100	$1.49

Exhibit 2-4: After Step 9, the tblOrderItem table should look like this

Unit 3

Complex queries

Complete this unit, and you'll know how to:

A Create outer join, inner join, and self-join queries; find non-matching records and duplicate records; and delete tables from a query.

B Create calculated fields in a query, and use the Expression Builder.

C Use queries to view summarized and grouped data from tables.

Topic A: Joining tables in queries

This topic covers the following Microsoft Office Specialist exam objectives for Access 2013.

#	Objective
3.1	**Create a query**
3.1.5	Create multi-table queries

Joins

Explanation

To run a query against two or more related tables, you need to specify an association between the fields in the tables. These associations are called *joins*. A join specifies how the data between tables is related. You can create the following types of joins:

- Outer joins (including Left and Right joins)
- Inner joins
- Self-joins

Joins are created automatically between related tables. The default join type is an *inner join*, which extracts data from two tables where the values of the joined fields match. To create a query using tables that are not related, you'll need to use Query Design view so you can define the join types.

Creating queries to join tables

To create queries that contain fields from one or more tables, you can use the Query Wizard. To start it, click the Query Wizard button on the Create tab. You then choose which type of query you want to create, such as a simple query. For example, to use the Simple Query Wizard, click the Query Wizard button on the Create tab, and select Simple Query Wizard in the New Query dialog box.

To create a query that joins tables:

1 Start the Simple Query Wizard.
2 From the Tables/Queries list, select the table on which you want to base the query.
3 Add the desired fields and click Next.
4 Add any other fields you want to include from other tables. Click Next.
5 Select the desired option for displaying your results, and click Next.
6 Enter a title for the query.
7 Select the desired option to either open the query or modify its design. Then click Finish to display the query results.

Do it!

A-1: Creating a query with the Simple Query Wizard

The files for this activity are in Student Data folder **Unit 3\Topic A**.

Here's how	Here's why
1 Open Operations1	From the current topic folder.
2 On the Create tab, click **Query Wizard**	The New Query dialog box opens with Simple Query Wizard selected.
Click **OK**	To start the Simple Query Wizard. You'll create a query that extracts and displays the Order ID and Order Date fields from tblOrder, and Product ID and Quantity from tblOrderItem.
3 From the Tables/Queries list, select **Table: tblOrder**	(If necessary.) You'll add fields from this table to the query.
4 In the Available Fields list, verify that **lngOrderID** is selected	You'll add this field to the query.
Click **>**	To add the field to the Selected Fields list. The lngOrderID field moves from the Available Fields list to the Selected Fields list.
Add **dtmOrdDate** to the Selected Fields list	Select dtmOrdDate in the Available Fields list and click Add.
5 From the Tables/Queries list, select **Table: tblOrderItem**	You'll add fields from this table to the query.
Add **strItemProductID** and **sngItemQuantity** to the Selected Fields list	Double-click them to add them quickly.
6 Click **Next**	
Verify that **Detail** is selected	To display the selected fields of every record in the query result.
7 Click **Next**	To move to the last page of the Wizard.
Edit the "What title do you want for your query?" box to read **qryProductsOrder**	To specify the title of the query.
Verify that the first option is selected	You'll view the results of this query as soon as you finish creating it.
8 Click **Finish**	To view the query results. They include the Order ID and Order Date fields from tblOrder, and the Product and Quantity fields from tblOrderItem. This query is an inner join.
9 Close the query	

Using Design view to create joins

Explanation

You can create and edit a join between tables in a query's Design view. If you have created a relationship between the tables in the Relationships window, Access will automatically display the join lines when you use the tables in a query. A *join line* indicates the join type and the relationship (if any) between the tables. If you have not created a relationship between the tables, you can still create joins for the query. In that case, one table should contain a field that can be related to a field in the other table.

A relationship you create just for a query or other object, but that isn't stored as a permanent relations ship, is sometimes referred to as an *ad hoc* relationship.

To create a query in Design view:

1 On the Create tab, click Query Design to open a new query and the Show Table dialog box.
2 On the Tables tab, from the list, select the table you want to include in the query, and click Add.
3 Add any other tables you want to include. Then click Close to close the Show Table dialog box.
4 From the list in the relevant cell of the Table row, select the table from which you want to include fields in the query.
5 From the list in the relevant cell of the Field row, select the field you want to include in the query.
6 Add any other necessary fields.

Do it!

A-2: Creating a join in Design view

Here's how	Here's why
1 On the Create tab, click **Query Design**	To open the Show Table dialog box. You'll create a query that will display the Product ID and Product Name fields from tblProduct, and the Order ID and Quantity fields from tblOrderItem.
Verify that the Tables tab is active	
2 From the list, select **tblProduct**	You'll add fields from this table to the query.
Click **Add**	To add this table to the query.
Double-click **tblOrderItem**	(In the Show Table dialog box.) To add it to the query.
Click **Close**	To close the Show Table dialog box.
Observe the top pane of the query	These two tables already have a one-to-many relationship, so you don't need to create an *ad hoc* relationship for the query.

3 Double-click the join line between tblProduct and tblOrderItem

The Join Properties dialog box appears. Because this is an inner join, option 1 is selected. It includes only rows where the joined fields from both tables contain the same value.

Click **Cancel**

To close the Join Properties dialog box.

4 In the Design grid, place the insertion point in the first cell of the Table row, as shown

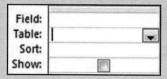

A drop-down arrow appears on the right side of the cell. Click the arrow to display a list of tables.

From the list, select **tblProduct**

You'll add a field from this table to the query.

5 Place the insertion point in the first cell of the Field row

You'll select a field from the list.

From the list, select **strProductID**

To add the field to the query. You can also double-click the field names to add them.

Place the insertion point in the first cell of the Sort row

From the list, select **Ascending**

To sort the results of the query in ascending order of product IDs.

Verify that **Show** is checked

6 Add **strProductName** from tblProduct

In the Table row, select the table name; in the Field row, select the field name.

Add **lngItemOrdID** and **sngItemQuantity** from tblOrderItem

7 Save the query as **qryOrdersProductNames**

8 On the Design tab, click **Run**

The query results display the product IDs, product names, order IDs, and quantities.

9 Close the query

Outer joins

Explanation

You use an *outer join* when you want your results to include rows that do not have a match in the joined table. In this case, the query results display empty cells in the unmatched record.

To create an outer join:

1 Start a new query in Design view.

2 Add the table from which you want to display all records.

3 Add the table that contains the related records, and add the fields you want to include in the query.

4 Double-click the join line between the two tables to open the Join Properties dialog box.

5 Select the desired option to display all of the records from one table and only the matching records from another table.

6 Click OK to close the Join Properties dialog box.

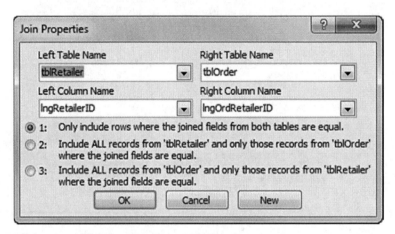

Exhibit 3-1: The Join Properties dialog box

Do it!   **A-3:   Creating an outer join**

Here's how	Here's why
1 Create a query in Design view	On the Create tab, click Query Design.
2 Add the tables **tblRetailer** and **tblOrder** to the query	(Close the Show Table dialog box when you finish adding the tables.) You'll create a query based on these tables. They have a one-to-many relationship.
3 Add **lngRetailerID** and **strRetailerName** from tblRetailer	Add them to the Design grid.
Add **lngOrderID** and **dtmOrdDate** from tblOrder	
From the Sort list for lngRetailerID, select **Ascending**	To sort the query results in ascending order by retailer ID.
4 Double-click the join line between tblRetailer and tblOrder	The Join Properties dialog box appears, as shown in Exhibit 3-1. The tables are related to each other based on the Retailer ID field.
Select the second option	To select all records from tblRetailer and only the matching records from tblOrder. This is a Left join.
Click **OK**	To set the properties and close the Join Properties dialog box.
5 Save the query as **qryOrdersByRetailers**	
6 Run the query	(Click the Run button on the Design tab.) The query results display all of the records from tblRetailer and only the matching records from tblOrder. This query is an outer join.
Observe the record for the retailer with ID 11	The Order ID and Order Date fields of this record are empty. This retailer has not placed any orders.
7 Close the query	

Joins including intermediate tables

Explanation

You can extract records from two tables that cannot be directly related—that is, they don't have fields that can be related. To do this, you need to use an intermediate table and create a many-to-many relationship between the two main tables. The intermediate table acts as a link between two tables that don't have related fields.

For example, a Retailers table and a Products table might have no related fields. Therefore, if you wanted to create a query showing which products a given retailer has ordered, you'd need to use the Order table as an intermediate, because the Order table contains both Retailer and Product fields.

To create a join by using an intermediate table:

1   Create a query in Design view.

2   Add the unrelated tables and the intermediate table.

3   Change the join properties between the tables as needed.

Do it!

A-4:   Creating a join with an intermediate table

Here's how	Here's why
1 Create a query in Design view	
Add **tblOrder, tblOrderItem,** and **tblProduct**	(Close the Show Table dialog box when you finish adding the tables.) The tblOrder and tblProduct tables have a many-to-many relationship. The tblOrderItem table serves as the intermediate table.
2 Add **lngOrderID** and **dtmOrdDate** from tblOrder	
Add **strProductID** and **strProductName** from tblProduct	
3 From the Sort list for lngOrderID, select **Ascending**	To sort the records in ascending order by order ID.
4 Double-click the join line between tblOrder and tblOrderItem	To open the Join Properties dialog box.
Select the third option	To include all of the records from tblOrderItem and only the matching records from tblOrder.
Click **OK**	To set the join properties.
5 Double-click the join line between tblOrderItem and tblProduct	
Select the third option	To include all records from tblOrderItem and only the matching records from tblProduct. This is a Right join.
Click **OK**	
6 Save the query as **qryOrderDetails**	
7 Run the query	
Observe the query results	The query results contain only the matching records from tblOrder and tblProduct. These fields are obtained by using tblOrderItem table as the intermediate table.
8 Close the query	

Self-join queries

Explanation

You can create a *self-join* by using two copies of the same table. A self-join is a query that displays matching records from the same table when there are matching values in two fields. For example, in the tblEmployee table, the Supervisor field contains the Employee ID of each employee's supervisor. You might want to see the last name of each employee's supervisor. To do this, you can create a self-join by joining the Supervisor field to the Employee ID field.

To create a self-join:

1 Create a query in Design view.

2 Add the table twice.

3 Create a relationship between the two copies of the table, based on the desired fields.

4 Add the fields.

Do it!

A-5: Creating a self-join query

Here's how	Here's why
1 Create a query in Design view	
2 Add **tblEmployee** twice	(Close the Show Table dialog box when you finish adding the tables.) Two copies of the same table appear. One table is named tblEmployee, and the other table is named tblEmployee_1.
Expand the height of the tables to display all fields	Drag the bottom edge of each table.
3 Drag **lngSupervisor** from tblEmployee and drop it on **lngEmpID** in tblEmployee_1	

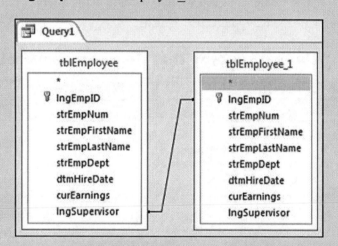

	A join line appears between tblEmployee and tblEmployee_1, joining the lngSupervisor field and the lngEmpID field in the same table.
4 In the Design grid, add **strEmpFirstName** and **strEmpLastName** from tblEmployee	
Add **strEmpLastName** from tblEmployee_1	
5 Save the query as **qrySupervisorDetails**	
6 Run the query	To see the query results. The third column displays the last name of each employee's supervisor.
7 Close the query	

Find-unmatched queries

To see the records in one table that don't have a matching record in another table, you can use a *find-unmatched query*. For example, you can use this type of query to find those retailers from the tblRetailer table who don't have any matching entries in the tblOrder table. You'd then know which retailers haven't placed any orders.

To create a find-unmatched query:

1 On the Create tab, click Query Wizard to open the New Query dialog box.
2 Select Find Unmatched Query Wizard and click OK.
3 Under View, select the desired option.
4 Select the database object from which you want to retrieve data. Click Next.
5 Under View, select the desired option. Select the database object to which you want to match the data, and click Next.
6 Select the matching fields from both tables, and click Next.
7 Add the fields that you want to include in the query results, and click Next.
8 Name the query and click Finish.

Do it!

A-6: Finding records that do not match between tables

Here's how	Here's why
1 Start the Query Wizard	Click Query Wizard on the Create tab.
2 Select **Find Unmatched Query Wizard**	
Click **OK**	To start the Find Unmatched Query Wizard.
3 Under View, verify that **Tables** is selected	
From the list, select **Table: tblRetailer**	To retrieve records from tblRetailer in the query results.
Click **Next**	To move to the next page of the wizard.
4 Under View, verify that **Tables** is selected	
5 In the list, select **Table: tblOrder**	To check for unmatched records in tblOrder.
Click **Next**	To move to the next page of the wizard.

6 In the first list, verify that
   lngRetailerID is selected

   In the second list, verify that
   lngOrdRetailerID is selected

   Click <=>   To specify that the records should be matched
                                               based on Retailer IDs in the tblRetailer and
                                               tblOrder tables. These two fields and the <=>
                                               operator appear beside "Matching fields" at the
                                               bottom of the wizard window.

   Click **Next**

7 Add **strRetailerName**,   Select each field name in the Available Fields
   strAddr1, **strAddr2**, and   list and click Add.
   strCity to the Selected Fields list

   Click **Next**   To move to the last page of the Find Unmatched
                                               Query Wizard.

8 Edit the name of the query to read
   qryRetailersWithoutOrders

   Click **Finish**   To display the query results.

   Observe the query results   It shows the record of the retailer who has not
                                               ordered any products.

9 Close the query

Finding duplicate records

Explanation
As a database grows and is used by multiple users, it inevitably acquires duplicate data. Some duplication is legitimate. For example, you may have customers with the same last name, or you may have orders that include the same products and amounts, but on different dates. Duplicate data is typically a problem if every field in the record is identical except for the primary key. For example, duplicate entries for the same customer, or the same order, should be eliminated.

The Find Duplicates Query Wizard can help eliminate duplicate data. To use this wizard:

1 On the Create tab, click Query Wizard.
2 In the New Query dialog box, select Find Duplicates Query Wizard and click OK.
3 Select the table or query you want to search. Click Next.
4 Select one or more fields to search for duplicate information. Click Next.
5 Select any other fields you want to show in the query, in addition to the duplicate data. Click Next.
6 Name the query and click Finish.

After using the Find Duplicates Query Wizard, examine the query results and determine whether the duplicates are legitimate or should be deleted from the database.

Do it!

A-7: Finding duplicate records

Here's how	Here's why
1 Start the Query Wizard	
Select **Find Duplicates Query Wizard**	
Click **OK**	To start the Find Duplicates Query Wizard.
2 Under View, verify that **Tables** is selected	To display a list of tables in this database.
From the list, select **Table: tblOrder**	If necessary.
Click **Next**	
3 Select **dtmOrdDate**	You'll search for identical orders that might have been placed on the same date.
Click **>**	To select dtmOrdDate as the duplicate-value field.
Click **Next**	
4 Click **>>**	To include all other fields from tblOrder in the query results. These other fields will help you decide if any duplicates are legitimate.
Click **Next**	
5 Edit the query name to read **qryDupOrders**	
Click **Finish**	The query results appear.
6 Examine the query results	Some order dates had multiple orders placed. But in each case, the Order ID and the Retailer number are unique, meaning that these are different orders.
Close the query	

Deleting tables from queries

Explanation

You can delete a table from a query. When you do so, any join lines that joined that table to another are also deleted. Any references to that table or its fields are removed from the query. (Deleting a table from a query does not remove it from the database.) Note that deleting a table from a query can produce unexpected results from the query and might render its results meaningless.

To delete a table from a query, open the query in Design view. In the upper pane, click the table to be removed and click Delete (or press the Delete key). You can also right-click the table and choose Remove Table.

Do it!

A-8: Deleting tables from a query

Here's how	Here's why
1 Open qryOrderDetails	You'll observe the effects of deleting a table from a query.
Observe the number of records in the status bar	This query returns 56 records.
Switch to Design view	
2 In the top pane of Design view, right-click **tblOrderItem** and choose **Remove Table**	The table disappears, as do the join lines that connected it to the other tables.
3 Run the query	
Observe the number of records in the status bar	There are now 528 records returned by this query. Without tblOrderItem to act as an intermediate table, the query returns each of the 24 records from tblProduct, within each of the 22 records from tblOrder (22 * 24 = 528). This is not a useful result.
4 Close the query	The Microsoft Office Access dialog box appears.
Click **No**	Do not save the changes to the query.
5 Reopen the query in Design view	The query opens in its original state.
6 Delete tblProduct from the upper pane	To remove this table from the query.
Observe the query design	When you deleted the table from the upper pane, the references to that table and its fields were deleted from the Design pane.
Run the query	The query also returns information that is not very useful.
Switch to Design view	

7 Add **strItemProductID** from tblOrderItem

Remove the sort from lngOrderID

Sort **strItemProductID** in Ascending order

Field:	lngOrderID	dtmOrdDate	strItemProductID
Table:	tblOrder	tblOrder	tblOrderItem
Sort:			Ascending

8 Point to the bar at the top of the strItemProductID column

You'll move this column so that it appears first in the query. (Don't point so high that the pointer changes to a large down-arrow.)

Press and hold the left mouse button

The pointer changes to an arrow with a box below it.

Drag the column to the left

Field:	lngOrderID	dtmOrdDate	strItemProductID
Table:	tblOrder	tblOrder	tblOrderItem
Sort:			Ascending

Until a black line appears to the left of the lngOrderID field.

Release the mouse

The strItemProductID field is now in the first column.

9 Run the query

For each Product ID, the query displays the order number and the date on which the product was ordered.

10 Update and close the query

11 Close the database

Topic B: Using calculated fields

This topic covers the following Microsoft Office Specialist exam objectives for Access 2013.

#	Objective
3.2	**Modify a Query**
3.2.6	Format fields within queries
3.3	**Utilize Calculated Fields and Grouping within a Query**
3.3.1	Add calculated fields
3.3.2	Add conditional logic

Creating calculated fields

Explanation

Calculated fields contain the result of calculations performed on other fields. For example, you might want to join the tblProduct and tblOrderItem tables to create a column that displays the sale amount of each order, but neither table has a Total Amount column.

You can calculate the sale amount by multiplying the values in the Unit Price column of the tblProduct table by the respective values in the Quantity column of the tblOrderItem table. You can create a query that includes the records you want from tblOrderItem and tblProduct, plus a calculated field called Amount. You specify this calculation in a cell in the Field row of the query.

Identical field names

When two tables have fields that use the same name, you must differentiate between them in formulas and expressions. For example, in this database, both tblOrderItem and tblProduct include a field named curUnitPrice. When this occurs, expressions must include the table name with the field name, separated by a period. The syntax is:

```
[tablename.fieldname]
```

The syntax for the calculation is:

```
Name_of_calculated_field: <Expression for calculation>
```

The name of the calculated field is followed by a colon (:) and the expression for the calculation. An expression specifies the field names and the calculation to be performed. `Name_of_calculated_field` appears as the field caption in the query result.

For example, examine the following expression:

```
Amt:[tblOrderItem.sngItemQuantity] * [tblProduct.curUnitPrice]
```

In this expression, the value in the Quantity field of the tblOrderItem table is multiplied by the value in the Unit Price field of the tblProduct table. `Amt` is the name of the calculated field, which is followed by a colon. In the expression for the calculation, `[tblOrderItem.sngItemQuantity]` refers to values in the Quantity field of the tblOrderItem table. You should always place the field names in square brackets ([ ]).

Including the table name in the first field (`[tblOrderItem.sngItemQuantity]`) is optional, because there is only one field named sngItemQuantity in the tables that are included in the query. Including the table name in the second field (`[tblProduct.curUnitPrice]`) is essential because there are two fields with that name. The expression would execute successfully and return the same results if it were written as:

```
Amt:[sngItemQuantity]*[tblProduct.curUnitPrice]
```

To promote accuracy, it is always best to include the table name with the field name in an expression, even when it's not strictly necessary.

To create a calculated field:

1   Create a query in Design view.
2   Add the desired tables and fields.
3   In the Field row, click the proper cell.
4   Enter the expression for the calculated field.

The Zoom box

You can use the Zoom box to more easily enter and edit long calculations. To open the Zoom box, right-click the field and choose Zoom. When you are done entering or editing the calculation, click OK to insert the calculation into the field.

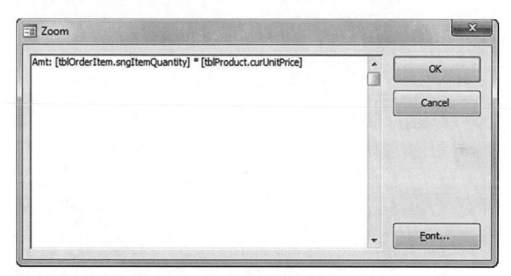

Exhibit 3-2: The Zoom box, with a long calculation

Do it!

B-1: Creating a calculated field

The files for this activity are in Student Data folder **Unit 3\Topic B**.

Here's how	Here's why
1 Open Operations2	From the current topic folder.
2 Create a query in Design view	
3 Add **tblOrderItem** and **tblProduct**	When you're done, close the Show Table dialog box.
4 Add **lngItemOrdID** and **sngItemQuantity** from tblOrderItem	
From the Sort list for lngItemOrdID, select **Ascending**	To sort the query results in ascending order by order ID.
5 Add **strProductName** from tblProduct	
6 Right-click in the fourth cell of the Field row and choose **Zoom**	The Zoom box lets you easily enter and see longer calculations. You can also enter calculations directly in the field to zoom.
Enter the following	This is a continuous line—don't press Enter.
`Amt: [tblOrderItem.sngItemQuantity] *` `  [tblProduct.curUnitPrice]`	
	The Zoom box should appear as shown in Exhibit 3-1.
Click **OK**	To create a calculated field, Amt, that multiplies the values in the Quantity field by corresponding values in the tblProduct table's version of the Unit Price field.
7 Double-click the join line between tblOrderItem and tblProduct	To open the Join Properties dialog box.
Select the third option	To display all records from tblOrderItem and only the matching records from tblProduct.
Click **OK**	
8 Save the query as **qryOrdersAndAmount**	
9 Run the query	To view the calculated field.

Modifying formats

Explanation

You can display the value in a calculated field as currency, a date, or a percentage. Format the value in the field by modifying the field's properties in the Property Sheet.

To format a displayed value:

1 Open the query in Design view.
2 Click in the field that contains the value you want to format.
3 Click the Property Sheet button on the Design tab. You can also right-click the field and choose Properties.
4 From the Format list in the Property Sheet, select the desired option.
5 From the Decimal Places list, select the desired option.
6 Close the Property Sheet and update the query.

Do it!

B-2: Changing the format of a displayed value

Here's how	Here's why
1 Switch to Design view	
2 Click in the fourth cell of the Field row	
On the Design tab, click [Property Sheet]	(If necessary.) To display the Property Sheet for the Amount field.
3 From the Format list, select **Currency**	To apply Currency formatting to the Amount field.
4 From the Decimal Places list, select **0**	No decimal values will appear in the cell.
Close the Property Sheet	
5 Run the query	To view the query results. The Amount field now appears in the currency format and contains no decimal places.

The Expression Builder

Explanation   You can use the Expression Builder to create expressions for a calculated field, to specify criteria for retrieving records, or to use conditional logic in a query. The Expression Builder creates expressions by using fields in tables and queries, built-in functions, and calculation operators, such as +, -, /, and *, as shown in Exhibit 3-3.

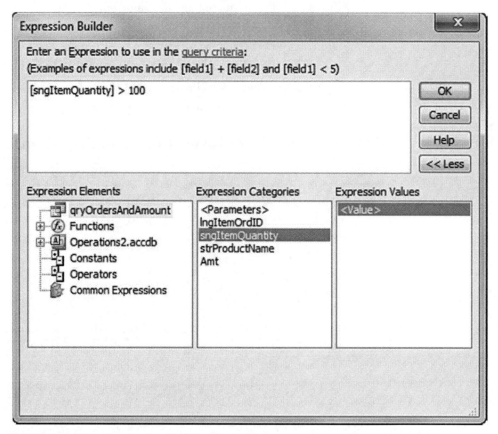

Exhibit 3-3: The Expression Builder dialog box

The Expression Builder contains two sections:

1   The upper section contains the Expression box, where you build the expression.

2   The lower section contains three boxes:

- The left-hand box contains folders listing the tables, queries, forms, and reports in the database, as well as folders containing functions, constants, operators, and expressions.

- The middle box lists the items contained in the folder selected on the left.

- The right-hand box displays any values for the items selected in the left and middle boxes.

Access uses an exclamation mark (!) to refer to a field in a table. For example, the expression that Access generates to refer to the sngItemQuantity field of the tblOrderItem table is:

```
[tblOrderItem]![sngItemQuantity]
```

To specify criteria by using the Expression Builder:

1   Open the desired query in Design view.

2   Click inside the proper cell of the Criteria row.

3   On the Design tab, click the Builder button to open the Expression Builder.

4   Create the desired criteria and click OK.

Do it!

B-3:   Using the Expression Builder

Here's how	Here's why
1 Switch to Design view	You'll use the Expression Builder to specify a criterion in this query.
2 Place the insertion point in the second cell of the Criteria row	
Click [🔖 Builder]	(In the Query Setup group on the Design tab.) To open the Expression Builder dialog box.
3 In the middle box, double-click **sngItemQuantity**	In the bottom section of the Expression Builder.
Observe the Expression box	It contains the field name.
4 Type **> 100**	Expression Builder Enter an Expression to use (Examples of expressions in [sngItemQuantity] > 100 (In the Expression box.) To specify that only the records in which Quantity is greater than 100 need to be displayed.
Click **OK**	To save the expression and close the Expression Builder dialog box.
5 Run the query	The query displays the orders and the calculated field. There are no records where Quantity is less than 100.
6 Update and close the query	
7 Close the database	

Topic C: Summarizing and grouping values

This topic covers the following Microsoft Office Specialist exam objectives for Access 2013.

#	Objective
3.1	**Create a query**
3.1.7	Delete queries

Creating summary functions

Explanation

Summary functions, such as Sum and Avg, perform calculations on a range of values to calculate an aggregate value. For example, to find the average sales of each product, you must first group the products together and then use the Avg function.

To create a query that displays summary values:

1 Create a query in Design view.
2 Add the desired table(s) and fields.
3 On the Design tab, click Totals.
4 In the relevant cell in the Totals row, select Group By for the necessary fields.
5 Create an expression using a summary function.
6 From the list in the proper cell of the Totals row, select Expression.
7 Save the query.

Do it!

C-1: Creating a query to display summary values

The files for this activity are in Student Data folder **Unit 3\Topic C**.

Here's how	Here's why
1 Open Operations3	
2 Create a query in Design view	
3 Add **tblOrder, tblOrderItem,** and **tblProduct**	You'll create summary values in the query based on these tables.
4 Add **lngOrderID** and **dtmOrdDate** from tblOrder	(In the Design grid.) You'll create a query that displays the total quantity of products ordered on a specific date, grouped by order ID.
Add **strProductName** from tblProduct	
5 Click **Totals**	(On the Design tab, in the Show/Hide group.) To display the Totals row in the Design grid. Group By appears in the cell. The data in the query result will be grouped based on Order ID.
6 Click in the fourth cell of the Field row	

7	Open the Expression Builder dialog box	(Click the Builder button on the Design tab.) You'll create a calculated field by using the Sum function.
8	Type **Total Quantity:**	(In the Expression box.) To specify the name of the calculated field.
9	In the left-hand box, double-click **Functions**	(In the bottom section of the Expression Builder.) Two options appear under the Functions folder.
10	Select **Built-In Functions**	You'll add a built-in function to the expression.
11	In the middle box, select **SQL Aggregate**	You'll have to scroll down.
12	In the right-hand box, double-click **Sum**	To add the function to the Expression box.
13	Delete **«Expr»**	

Total Quantity: «Expr» Sum(«expression»)

		From the Expression box.
14	Edit the expression as indicated	

Total Quantity: Sum([tblOrderItem]![sngItemQuantity])

		This expression will calculate the total quantity of a product ordered.
	Click **OK**	To save the expression.
15	Click in the fourth cell of the Total row	
	From the list, select **Expression**	To specify that this field is an expression field.
16	In the second cell of the Criteria row, enter **#06-Jan-13#**	To specify that the query results contain only the records for orders placed on the date January 6, 2013.
17	Save the query as **qryQuantityOnDate**	
18	Run the query	The query results appear. Each record displays the total quantity of products ordered January 6, 2013, grouped by Order ID.
	Close the query	

Concatenation

Explanation

You can combine values from different fields into one field. This process is called *concatenation*. For example, you can use the Expression Builder to create an expression that concatenates the values in the First Name and Last Name fields of the tblEmployee table, as follows:

```
[tblEmployee]![strEmpFirstName]&(' ')&
[tblEmployee]![strEmpLastName]
```

In this expression, `&(' ')&` ensures that a space appears between the first and last names of the employee. The `strEmpFirstName` and `strEmpLastName` in the expression are the names of the First Name and Last Name fields, respectively, in the tblEmployee table.

Note: The plus (+) sign can also be used to concatenate strings, but it can produce unexpected results when you're concatenating strings that start with numbers.

Do it!

C-2: Using queries to concatenate values

Here's how	Here's why
1 Create a query in Design view	
2 Add **tblEmployee**	Close the Show Table dialog box when you finish adding the table.
3 Add **lngEmpID** and **strEmpNum**	
4 Click in the third cell of the Field row	
5 Open the Expression Builder dialog box	You'll create a concatenated field.
6 Create the expression as shown	Name:[tblEmployee]![strEmpFirstName] & ' ' & [tblEmployee]![strEmpLastName]
	To concatenate the first name, a space, and the last name in one field.
Click **OK**	To save the expression.
7 Save the query as **qryEmployeeNames**	
8 Run the query	
Observe the Name field	The Name field now contains the contents of both the First Name and Last Name fields rendered as a single string, separated by a space for readability.
9 Select **qrySupervisorDetails**	In the Navigation pane. You'll delete this query.
Press DELETE	The Microsoft Access dialog box appears.
Click **Yes**	To confirm the deletion. The query is removed from the database.
10 Close the database	

Unit summary: Complex queries

Topic A   In this topic, you learned how to create a query by using multiple tables. You used the Simple Query Wizard to **join tables**. You also created queries in Design view. You created an outer join, an inner join, and a self-join. You also displayed the records that do not match between tables by using the **Find Unmatched Query Wizard**. Next, you learned how to find potential duplicate records by using the **Find Duplicates Query Wizard**. Finally, you learned how to **delete tables** from a query.

Topic B   In this topic, you learned how to create **calculated fields** by entering an expression in Design view. You also formatted the value of a calculated field by using the **Property Sheet**. Additionally, you created calculated fields by using the **Expression Builder** dialog box.

Topic C   In this topic, you learned how to group records and display summarized fields. You used **summary functions**, such as Sum and Avg, to display summarized values. You also learned how to **concatenate** and display the values in more than one field by using the Expression Builder dialog box.

Review questions

1 What must be created before you can create a query for two or more tables?

2 Which of the following is the default join type?

   A Outer join

   B Self-join

   C Inner join

   D There is no default join type.

3 Which Access wizard is used to create a query that joins two tables?

4 Which Access wizard is used to find records that do not have matching records in another table?

5 In the syntax for calculated fields, what character is used to separate the field name from the expression?

6 Which Access feature is useful for creating calculated fields?

Independent practice activity

In this activity, you'll create queries by using multiple tables and different types of joins. Then, you'll create a calculated field that shows the total number of orders placed by a retailer. Finally, you'll create a query that concatenates fields from a database table.

The files for this activity are in Student Data folder **Unit 3\Unit summary**.

1 Open OperationsIPA.

2 Using the tblRetailer, tblOrder, and tblOrderItem tables, create a query that displays these fields: Retailer ID, Retailer Name, Order ID, Order Date, Product ID, and Quantity. Save the query as **qryRetailerOrders**.

3 Using the tblProduct and tblOrderItem tables, create an outer join where all product IDs from tblProduct and only the matching records from tblOrderItem appear in the query results. Name the query **qryProductOrders**.

4 Use the tblOrder and tblRetailer tables to create a query that displays Retailer ID, Retailer Name, and a calculated field called **Orders** showing the number of orders placed by a retailer. (*Hint:* Use the Count function with lngOrderID as the argument in the Expression Builder.) Save the query as **qryTotalOrders**.

5 Create a query called **qryMailingList** that displays the Address1, City, Region, and ZIP Code fields of the tblRetailer table, separated by commas, in a single field.

6 Close the database.

Unit 4

Advanced form design

Complete this unit, and you'll know how to:

A Add unbound controls to a form, change the tab order of controls, group controls, and format a form for printing.

B Use controls to add graphics to a form.

C Use controls to add calculated fields to a form.

D Add a combo box to a form.

E Create multiple-item forms, split forms, datasheet forms, subforms, and navigation forms.

Topic A: Adding unbound controls

This topic covers the following Microsoft Office Specialist exam objectives for Access 2013.

#	Objective
4.3	**Format a Form**
4.3.1	Modify tab order in forms
4.3.2	Format print layouts
4.3.5	Change margins
4.3.7	Auto-order forms

Using unbound controls

Explanation

You can use unbound controls in a form to display text, rectangles, lines, or images. *Unbound controls* are controls that are not linked to any external data sources, such as fields in tables. In contrast, a *bound control* is directly tied to the source data: if you change the data in the field, the control changes, and if you change the control, the data in the field changes.

An example of an unbound control is a *label control*, which describes the data contained in another control. Most controls on a typical form are unbound. Many controls can be bound or unbound. For instance, a check box might be bound to a true/false field in a table. Likewise, a text box can be bound to a field, but it doesn't have to be.

Even though a control is unbound, it can still affect a table. For instance, a command button might add a new record and fill in the fields with default values, but it is not bound to the data.

A note about forms and reports

Although this topic is primarily about forms, most of the functions relating to controls are used the same way in reports, which can contain the same controls as forms.

Rectangles

The simplest controls are shapes used for design and organization. For instance, you can draw rectangles on your forms and reports to logically group controls or to add a border. To do so, open the form or report in Design view. On the Design tab, select the Rectangle control in the Controls group. Then drag to draw the rectangle on the form or report.

Do it!

A-1:   Drawing a rectangle around a control

The files for this activity are in Student Data folder **Unit 4\Topic A**.

Here's how	Here's why
1 Open ProductOrders1	From the current topic folder.
2 Open frmProduct	The form header contains a heading for the report. You'll draw a rectangle around the heading.
3 Switch to Design view	The Design, Arrange, and Format tabs appear, under Form Design Tools, on the ribbon.
4 On the Design tab, open the Controls gallery Select the Rectangle control, as shown	
5 Drag to create a rectangle around **Outlander Spices**, as shown	

6 Switch to Form view	You'll see the rectangle around Outlander Spices.
7 Switch to Design view	The rectangle you drew is still selected.
8 On the Design tab, click **Property Sheet**	(If necessary.) To display the Property Sheet for the rectangle, which should still be selected.
Click the **Format** tab	If necessary.
From the Border Width list, select **2 pt**	
Close the Property Sheet	
9 Switch to Form view	The rectangle around Outlander Spices now has a thicker border.
10 Update and close the form	

Tab order

Explanation

As the user tabs through a form, controls are selected based on the specified *tab order*. By default, the tab order is determined by the order in which the controls were created and placed on the form. Each new control is last in the tab order. You can change the tab order or set controls to be skipped when a user tabs through the form. If you use interactive controls on a report, you can change the tab order in exactly the same way.

As an alternative, you can use the Auto Order option to set the order to be left-to-right and top-to-bottom.

To change the tab order:

1 Open the form (or report) in Design view.
2 On the Design tab, click Tab Order to open the Tab Order dialog box.
3 Under Section, select the desired option.
4 Under Custom Order, select the field for which you want to change the tab order.
5 Drag the field up or down in the list. Then click OK.

To auto-order a form:

1 Open the form (or report) in Design view.
2 Open the Tab Order dialog box.
3 Click Auto Order.
4 Click OK.

Do it!

A-2: Changing the tab order

Here's how	Here's why
1 Open frmOrder	
2 Verify that the insertion point is in the Order ID field	You'll test the tab order of the controls in this form.
Press (TAB)	The insertion point moves to the Notes field.
Press (TAB) again	The insertion point moves to the Order Date field.
Press (TAB) again	The insertion point moves to the Order ID field.
3 Switch to Design view	You'll change the tab order of the controls.

4 On the Design tab, click **Tab Order**	(In the Tools group.) To open the Tab Order dialog box.
Under Custom Order, select **dtmOrdDate**	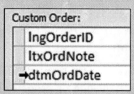
	(Click the gray box to the left of dtmOrdDate.) You'll move this field up in the tab order.
Drag **dtmOrdDate** up and drop it between IngOrderID and ltxOrdNote, as shown	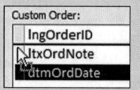
	(Drag the box.) As you drag, a thick line indicates where the name will be dropped.
5 Click **OK**	To close the Tab Order dialog box and set the new tab order.
6 Switch to Form view	The insertion point is in the Order ID field.
Press (TAB) twice	The insertion point moves according to the new tab order.
7 Switch to Design view	You'll reset the tab order.
Click **Tab Order**	
Rearrange the tab order to a random order	Under Custom Order, drag the fields up or down.
Click **OK**	To close the dialog box.
8 Switch to Form view	
Test the tab order	The insertion point moves somewhat randomly between the fields.
9 Switch to Design view	You'll use Auto Order to set the tab order.
Click **Tab Order**	
10 Click **Auto Order**	The tab order now runs from top to bottom.
Test the new tab order	Switch to Form view and tab through the form.
11 Update the form	

Grouped controls

Explanation

Grouped controls are two or more controls placed in a group. You generally organize related controls into a group. You can create grouped controls if you need to change the properties of multiple controls simultaneously or you want to arrange the controls on a form.

To modify the properties of all of the controls in the group, you can select the group and then change its properties, instead of changing each control's properties individually. For example, if you need to change the font of some fields on a form, you can group these fields and change the font for the entire group.

To create grouped controls, open the form in Design view and select the desired controls on the form. Then, on the Form Design Tools | Arrange tab, click the Size/Space button and choose Group.

To modify a group's properties, right-click the grouped control and use the shortcut menu.

Do it!

A-3: Grouping controls

Here's how	Here's why
1 Switch to Design view	You'll group the controls on this form.
2 Select the label control for **Order ID**	To add this control to the group.
Press (SHIFT)	You'll select more controls to add to the group.
Select the text box control for **lngOrderID**	(Continue to hold the Shift key down.) To add this control to the group.
Select the label control for **Order Date**	Keep the Shift key down.
3 Select the text box control for **dtmOrderDate**	
Release (SHIFT)	Four controls are now selected. (The associated labels are selected, but they might not have a box around them.)
4 On the Arrange tab, click [Size/Space]	
Choose **Group**	

5	Point to one of the two text boxes	
		The pointer changes to a four-headed arrow.
6	Drag slightly to the right	The grouped controls move as a unit.
	Click ⤺	(The Undo button is on the Quick Access toolbar.) To undo the change.
7	Right-click the border of a text box	To display the shortcut menu for the grouped controls.
	Choose **Properties**	The Property Sheet's Selection type is "Multiple selection." You'll change a group property.
	Click the **Format** tab	If necessary.
8	Click **Back Color**	To set this property for the grouped controls.
	Click ⋯	(The Build button appears next to the Back Color box.) To open the Color dialog box.
9	In the Color dialog box, click **Yellow**	
		To set the background color of the grouped controls to yellow.
	Observe the Back Color box	It displays the hexadecimal value for the selected color.
10	Close the Property Sheet	
11	Switch to Form view	The grouped controls have a yellow background color.
12	Update and close the form	

Control arrangement by table

Explanation
You can arrange controls in a table. In this case, the term table refers to the layout, not to a data table. The process is the same for controls in forms and reports.

Once the controls are in a table, you can manipulate it like a table in a Word document; you can select whole rows or columns, insert columns, split and merge cells, move rows, or move the whole table. You can also draw gridlines around cells and set the padding between cells.

To use table functions, do this:

1 Open or create a form or report in Design view.
2 Select the controls you want in a table.
3 On the Arrange tab, click Stacked or Tabular. Stacked puts all controls in the details sections, while Tabular puts labels in the header and fields in the details.

Do it!

A-4: Arranging controls in tables

The files for this activity are in Student Data folder **Unit 4\Topic A**.

Here's how	Here's why
1 Open frmRetailer in Design view	You'll arrange the controls in table format.
2 Press (CTRL) + (A)	To select all controls.
3 On the Arrange tab, click **Stacked**	In the Table group. This will arrange the controls in a table. You can select rows and columns in this table.
4 Click **Control Margins**, **Narrow**	(In the Position group.) Control margins sets the margin around the text within the control.
5 Click **Control Padding**, **Wide**	The controls in the table are spaced widely.
Click **Control Padding**, **Narrow**	To space the cells more closely.
6 Point to the middle of any cell	So the pointer is a four-headed arrow.
Drag the table slightly down and to the right	The entire table moves.
7 Point to the top of the field column so the pointer changes to a heavy black arrow and click	To select the column.
8 On the Arrange tab, click **Insert Left**	A blank column is inserted to the left of the selected column.
9 Select the blank column	(Point to the top and click.) The empty cells are selected.

10	Click **Merge**	(In the Merge/Split group.) To merge all the cells in the selected column into one.
11	Click **Split Vertically**	To split the middle column and select the top cell.
12	Click **Select Column**	(In the Rows & Columns group.) Another way to select a column. Both cells are selected.
	Press (DELETE)	To remove the blank column
13	Select the **Retailer Name** label	
	On the Arrange tab, click **Select Row**	
	Click **Move Up**	To move the row up in the table. Now the retailer name is at the top.
14	Switch to Form view	To see the results.
	Close the form without saving changes	

Form printing

Explanation

Although reports are usually better suited for printing Access database information, you can also print forms. Before doing so, you can configure the form to make the printed output easier to read. You may also want to delete any sensitive or confidential information from the form before it is printed.

To format the page layout, do this:

1 Open a form in Design view.
2 Arrange the controls on the form to support a printed format.
3 Choose File, Print, Print Preview to switch to Print Preview.
4 Use the controls in the Page Size and Page Layout groups to format the page layout, or click Page Layout to see all of the controls in one dialog box.
5 Save the form.

A-5: Formatting the page layout

The files for this activity are in Student Data folder **Unit 4\Topic A**.

Here's how	Here's why
1 Create a form from **tblEmployee**	Select the table. Then, on the Create tab, click Form.
Choose **File**, **Print**, **Print Preview**	The information is there, but the results are not very visually appealing.
Switch to Design view	(Right-click the form tab and choose Design view.) You'll format the form for printing.
Save the form as **frmEmployee**	
2 Display the Property Sheet	
Rename the form **Employees**	Click on the heading text box and change the Caption field in the Property Sheet.
Change the Width of the header text box to **1.25**, as shown	
3 Point to the top edge of the **lngEmpID** text box, as shown	The pointer changes to a solid black arrow.
Click the top edge of the text box	To select the entire column of text boxes.
In the Property Sheet, on the Format tab, change the Width to **1.8**	To reduce the size of the text boxes. This should be wide enough for last names.
4 On the Property Sheet, from the Selection type drop-down box, select **Form**	To select the form itself.
Set the Width of the form to **3.1**	
5 Return to Print Preview	Click File, Print, Print Preview.

6	Click **Margins**, **Wide**	(In the Page Size group.) To make the margins more suitable for a printed page.
	Select **Print Data Only**	The title, record shading, and text labels are all hidden, leaving only the data fields. This isn't the look you want for this form; you'll change it back.
	Clear **Print Data Only**	The hidden items are displayed again.
7	Click **Page Setup**	The Page Setup dialog box appears. The Print Options tab appears by default. The Page Setup includes some of the controls seen on the ribbon.
	Select the **Page** tab	This tab includes more print controls.
	Select the **Columns** tab	This tab sets up columns on the printed page.
8	Edit the Number of Columns box to **2**	Now that the text boxes are narrower, you can make better use of page real estate (and use less paper) by displaying the data in columns.
	Under Column Layout, choose **Down, then Across**	To format the entries on the page in columns instead of rows.
	Click **OK**	To save the changes and close the Page Setup dialog box.
9	Observe the form	The page layout is better suited to a printed form. You'll make one more change.
10	Switch to Design view	The fields include salary data, which is sensitive personal information. Since you don't know what might happen to the printed version of this form after it leaves your hands, you'll remove the salary data.
	Delete the **curEarnings** text box	
11	Switch to Print Preview	The salary data is no longer included.
12	Update and close the form	
	Close the database	

Topic B: Graphics

This topic covers the following Microsoft Office Specialist exam objectives for Access 2013.

#	Objective
4.3	**Format a Form**
4.3.6	Insert backgrounds
4.3.9	Insert images

Image controls

Explanation

You can add graphics to a form by using either an image control or an unbound object frame control. An *image control* is an unbound control. It cannot be edited after you insert it in the form, but you can resize it.

To add an image to a form:

1   Open the form in Design view.
2   In the Controls group on the Design tab, choose Insert Image, Browse.
3   Select the image file and click OK.
4   Draw the image control on the form. The image is inserted in the frame you draw.

After you insert an image, it remains available in a gallery of images the next time you click the Insert Image control.

Do it!

B-1:   Adding an image to a form

The files for this activity are in Student Data folder **Unit 4\Topic B**.

Here's how	Here's why
1 Open ProductOrders2	From the current topic folder.
2 Open frmRetailer in Design view	You'll add a graphic to this form.
3 On the Design tab, beside the Controls gallery, choose **Insert Image**, **Browse**	The Insert Picture dialog box opens.
From the drop-down beside the **File Name** box, select **All Files**	If necessary.
Select **Spices-2**	From the current topic folder.
Click **OK**	To select the image an close the Insert Picture dialog box. The pointer changes to an Image Control icon.
4 Point as shown	
Drag as shown	When you release the mouse button, the image is inserted in the frame you drew.

5 Click **Insert Image**

Logo
Title
Insert Image ▾
Date

Image Gallery

Spices-2

Browse...

The image you selected is now loaded in an image gallery that appears above the Browse button.

6 Switch to Form view

The image appears on the form.

7 Update the form

Logos

Explanation

You can add a corporate logo to the Header section of a form.

To embed a logo image in the Header:

1 Open the form in Design view.

2 On the Design tab, in the Header/Footer group, click Logo. The Insert Image dialog box appears.

3 Navigate to and select the logo file, and click OK. An image object is inserted in the Header section of the form, with the logo image in it.

4 Resize the image object as needed.

Do it!

B-2:   Embedding a logo in a form header

The files for this activity are in Student Data folder **Unit 4\Topic B**.

Here's how	Here's why
1 Switch to Design view	
2 Expand the Form Header section by dragging the Detail bar down, as shown	
	You'll insert an unbound object frame control in the Form Header section.
3 In the Header/Footer group, click ![Logo]	(The Logo button.) The Insert Picture dialog box opens.
From the drop-down beside the **File Name** box, select **All Files**	If necessary.
Select **logo**	From the current topic folder.
Click **OK**	To select the image an close the Insert Picture dialog box. The logo is inserted in the header in an image frame.
4 Select the image frame	
Point to the lower-right corner of the image frame	The pointer changes to double-headed arrow.
5 Drag down and to the right	
	To expand the logo image in the header.
6 Switch to Form view	
Update and close the form	

Background pictures

Explanation

You can add a picture to the background of the form or report, without using an image control. You can link or embed a background image. If you link an image, the background will reload the image from the source file every time to open the form. If you embed, a copy of the image is saved with the form. Much like a Windows desktop background, you can choose to center, stretch, or tile the image.

To add a background image to a form or report:

1 In the property sheet, click the Picture value.
2 Click the Browse button.
3 Navigate to the image you want, select it, and click OK.

You can also add a background image by in Design view by clicking the Background Image button on the Format tab and navigating to the image you want, but you'll still need to use the property sheet to change the picture properties.

Do it!

B-3: Adding a background image to a form

Here's how	Here's why
1 Open frmProductOrder in Design view	
Open the property sheet for the form	If necessary.
2 On the Format tab in the Property Sheet, verify the Picture Type is Embedded	
Set Picture Tiling to **No**	
Set Picture Size Mode to **Stretch**	
3 Click on Picture, then click [⋯]	The Browse button.
Navigate to the current topic folder	
Select **Spices-2** and click **OK**	The image appears as the form background.
4 Switch to Form view	The picture takes up the entire form area.
5 Close the form	Don't save changes.
6 Close the database	

Topic C: Adding calculated values

Explanation

You can bind a form control to a calculated field in a query, a report, or another form by using the control's Property Sheet.

To bind a control to a calculated field:

1 Open the form in Design view.
2 In the Controls group, click Text Box.
3 Draw the control on the form.
4 Select the control, click Property Sheet, and click the Data tab in the Property Sheet.
5 From the Control Source list, select the calculated field.
6 Close the Property Sheet.

You can also use a control's Property Sheet to change its formatting.

Do it!

C-1: Binding a control to a calculated field

The files for this activity are in Student Data folder **Unit 4\Topic C**.

Here's how	Here's why
1 Open ProductOrders3	From the current topic folder.
2 Open frmProductOrder in Design view	This form is based on the qryProductOrder query. You'll bind a control in this form to a calculated field in the query.
3 On the Design tab, click the Text Box control button	 You'll insert a text box control in the form.
4 Draw the control as shown	
Observe the window	A label control has been added to the form, along with the text box control.
5 Click the label control	
6 Display the Property Sheet for the label control	
7 Edit the Caption box to read **Order Amount**	Leave the Property Sheet open.
Arrange and resize the label control	To line it up with the other labels and to display the complete text.

8	Click the text box control	"Unbound" appears in the text box. The properties for this text box appear in the Property Sheet.
9	In the Property sheet, click the **Data** tab	To display data-related properties.
	From the Control Source list, select **Amount**	

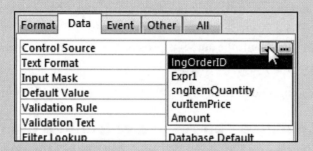

		You'll bind the control to this calculated field.
10	In the Property Sheet, click the **Format** tab	
	From the Format list, select **Currency**	
	Close the Property Sheet	The text box is now linked to Amount, the calculated field in the qryProductOrder query.
11	Switch to Form view	The contents of the calculated field appear in the text box control.
12	Update and close the form	

Calculated controls

Explanation

To create a *calculated control*, you write the expression to be evaluated directly in the Control Source box on the Data tab of the control's Property Sheet. This control resembles a calculated field in a query, but the form does the calculating. For example, to display the value of a sales transaction in a control, enter the following expression:

```
=[sngItemQuantity]*[curUnitPrice]
```

The control then uses this expression as its data source.

To create a calculated control:

1 Open the form in Design view.
2 In the Controls group, click the Text Box button.
3 Place the control on the form.
4 Display the control's Property Sheet.
5 In the Control Source box on the Data tab, enter the expression needed to perform the calculation.
6 Close the Property Sheet.

Aligning controls

You can align two or more controls to the right, left, top, or bottom. You can also align controls to a form's Design grid. To align controls on a form:

1 Open the form in Design view or Layout view.
2 Select the desired controls.
3 On the Arrange tab, use the alignment tools in the Sizing & Ordering group.

Do it!

C-2: Creating a calculated control

Here's how	Here's why
1 Open frmOrderItem in Design view	You'll add a calculated control to this form.
2 Expand the Detail section enough to easily fit another text box and label	Drag the Form Footer bar down.
3 Add a text box control	

Unit Price	curUnitPrice
Text16:	Unbound

A corresponding label control also appears.

| 4 Edit the caption for the new label to read **Amount** | In the Property Sheet for the control. |

5	Select the new text box control	Its properties will appear in the Property Sheet.
	In the Control Source box, enter **=[sngItemQuantity]*[curUnitPrice]**	
		(On the Data tab.) To display the sale amount of each transaction in this field.
	From the Format list, select **Currency**	On the Format tab in the Property Sheet.
	From the Decimal Places list, select **2**	
	Close the Property Sheet	
6	Switch to Form view	The calculated data appears in the new text box control. The Amount label is not aligned properly with the other controls.
7	Switch to Design view	You'll align the Amount label control with the Unit Price control.
8	Select the Unit Price label control	
	While holding (SHIFT), select the **Amount** label control	Holding Shift allows you to select multiple controls.
9	On the Arrange tab, click **Align** and choose **Left**	(In the Sizing & Ordering group.) To align the controls to the left. Amount is now aligned with the other label controls.
10	Update the form	
11	Switch to Form view	All of the label controls are aligned to the left.
12	Close the form	
	Close the database	

Topic D: Adding combo boxes

This topic covers the following Microsoft Office Specialist exam objectives for Access 2013.

#	Objective
4.3	**Format a Form**
4.3.10	Modify existing forms

Adding a combo box to a form

Explanation

A *combo box* control displays values in a drop-down list. Users can also type in a value. You can modify the properties of the combo box.

To add a combo box to a form:

1 Open the form in Design view.

2 On the Design tab, click the Combo Box button.

3 Draw the control on the form. The Combo Box Wizard appears.

4 To use the combo box to extract data from tables or queries, select the first option. Click Next.

5 Select the desired database object. Click Next.

6 In the Available Fields list, select the field whose values will be listed in the combo box. Add it to the Selected Fields list. Click Next.

7 Select a sort order for the list (if necessary) and click Next.

8 Adjust the column width (if necessary) and click Next.

9 Select "Store that value in this field" and select the field where you want to store the value that is selected in the combo box. Click Next.

10 Enter a label name for the combo box, and click Finish.

Do it!

D-1: Adding a combo box to a form

The files for this activity are in Student Data folder **Unit 4\Topic D**.

Here's how	Here's why
1 Open ProductOrders4	
2 Open frmOrder in Design view	You'll add a combo box to this form.
3 In the Controls group, click the Combo Box control button	
4 Draw the combo box control, as shown	dtmOrdDate / txOrdNote The Combo Box Wizard appears.

5	Verify that the first option is selected	To use this combo box to extract values from a field in a table or a query.
	Click **Next**	
6	Under View, verify that **Tables** is selected	
	From the list, select **Table: tblRetailer**	You'll extract data from the tblRetailer table.
	Click **Next**	
7	Add **strRetailerName** to the Selected Fields list	The values from this field will be listed in the combo box.
	Click **Next**	On this wizard page, you can choose to sort the records.
	Click **Next**	This page displays the data in the Retailer Name column. You can modify the column width.
8	Click **Next**	Here, you can specify where the value selected in the combo box should be stored.
9	Select **Store that value in this field**	You'll bind the control to a field in the table.
	From the list, select **lngOrdRetailerID**	To bind the control to the lngOrdRetailerID field.
	Click **Next**	On this page, you can enter a label for the combo box.
10	Edit the label box to read **Retailer Name**	
	Click **Finish**	To add the combo box to the form.
11	Align the Retailer Name label control with the Notes label control	Select the Retailer Name label control and the control below it. On the Arrange tab, click Align and choose Left.
12	Update the form	
13	Switch to Form view	
14	Click the drop-down arrow for the Retailer Name list	A list of retailer names appears.
	Close the list	Click anywhere on the form.

Changing combo box properties

Explanation   After you create a combo box, you can modify its properties. To do so:

1   In Design view, select the combo box.
2   Display its Property Sheet.
3   Modify the properties as needed.
4   Close the Property Sheet.

Do it!   ## D-2:   Modifying the properties of a combo box

Here's how	Here's why
1 Switch to Design view	
2 Open the combo box control's Property Sheet	Select the combo box and click Property Sheet on the Design tab.
On the Other tab, edit the Name box to read **Retailer Name**	To specify a new name for the combo box.
On the Data tab, in the Default Value box, enter **8**	To specify that the eighth item in the list is the default value.
Close the Property Sheet	
3 Switch to Form view	
4 Click [▶]	(The New Blank Record button is in the status bar.) You'll observe the Retailer ID for a new record.
Observe the form	The Retailer Name field automatically displays Spice Hall (the eighth name in the list), indicating that it is the combo box's default value.
5 Update and close the form	
6 Close the database	

Topic E: Advanced form types

This topic covers the following Microsoft Office Specialist exam objectives for
Access 2013.

#	Objective
1.3	**Navigate through a database**
1.3.1	Set a form as the startup option
1.3.3	Use navigation forms

Multiple-item forms

Explanation

Although most forms display only one record at a time, you can create multiple-item
forms, which display multiple records. Multiple-item forms resemble datasheets in
Access, but forms can be customized with graphics, buttons, and other form objects.

To create a multiple-item form:

1. In the Navigation Pane, select the table from which the form will be created.
2. Click the Create tab.
3. In the Forms group, click Multiple Items. A multiple-item form is created.
4. Format the form as needed, and save it.

Do it!

E-1: Creating a multiple-item form

The files for this activity are in Student Data folder **Unit 4\Topic E**.

Here's how	Here's why
1 Open ProductOrders5	From the current topic folder.
2 Click **tblRetailer**	To select the table. You'll create a multiple-item form.
3 Click the **Create** tab	
Click **More Forms** and choose **Multiple Items**	(In the Forms group.) A multiple-item form opens in Layout view.
4 Save the form as **frmMultiRetailer**	
Close the Property Sheet	If necessary.
5 Point to the bottom border of the **Retailer ID** field	The pointer changes to a double-headed arrow.
Drag up	
	Drag until the field is approximately half of its original height. When you do this, all rows change to the same height.
6 Reduce the width of the Retailer ID field	
	Point to the right border until the pointer becomes a double-headed arrow; then drag to the left until the field is just large enough for its heading. When you do this, all cells in the column change to this width.
7 Adjust the width of the rest of the fields	Point to the right border of each field and drag left to fit the contents.
8 At the top of the form, triple-click **tblRetailer**	To make the field editable and select the title.
Edit the name of the form to read **Retailers**	
9 Update and close the form	

Split forms

Explanation

A *split form* displays both a form view and a datasheet view of the same data. Both views are editable. You can use the datasheet view to perform searches and to navigate, and use the form view to display and update individual records.

To create a split form:

1 In the Navigation Pane, select the table from which the form will be created.
2 Click the Create tab.
3 In the Forms group, click Split Form. A split form opens in Layout view, as shown in Exhibit 4-1.
4 Save the form to make it editable.
5 Format the form as needed, and save it again.

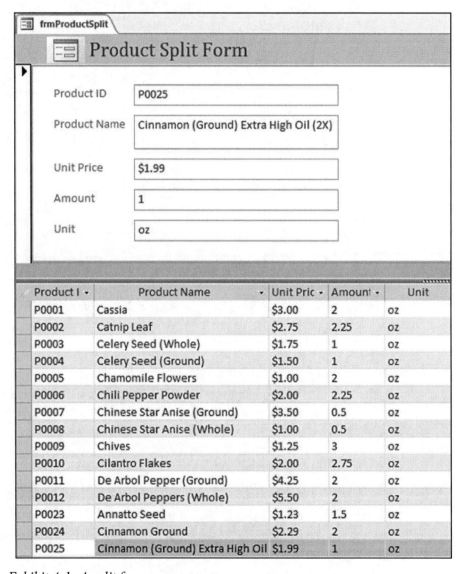

Exhibit 4-1: A split form

Do it!

E-2:   **Creating a split form**

Here's how	Here's why
1 Click **tblProduct**	(In the Navigation Pane.) You'll create a split form based on this table.
2 Click the **Create** tab	If necessary.
3 Click **More Forms** and choose **Split Form**	(In the Forms group.) A split form opens in Layout view.
4 Save the form as **frmProductSplit**	
Edit the form title to read **Product Split Form**	Triple-click the title to make it editable.
5 Reduce the size of the top form	Point to the border between the forms. When the pointer changes to a double-headed arrow, drag up.
6 Reduce the size of the fields in the top form	Select all five fields and drag the right border to the left.
7 Click ▶	(The Next Record button is in the status bar at the bottom of the form.) To navigate to the next record in the form.
Navigate to Product ID **P0025**	(The 15th record.) This is the longest Product Name in the table.
Adjust the width of the fields in the top form to fit the name	(If necessary.) Drag the borders of the Product Name field. The form should now resemble Exhibit 4-1.
8 Update and close the form	

Datasheet forms

Explanation

A datasheet form resembles a split form. But while a split form displays different views of the same data, a datasheet form displays data from different sources, such as two tables. A datasheet form is typically used when two tables have a one-to-many relationship.

You can create a datasheet form from a table that has a one-to-many relationship with another table. In the Navigation Pane, select a table that has a one-to-many relationship with another table. On the Create tab, click Form. A form opens in Layout view. It contains a datasheet that shows the data from the other table, as shown in Exhibit 4-2.

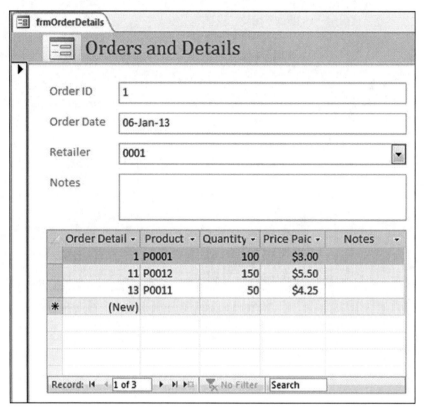

Exhibit 4-2: A datasheet form

Do it!

E-3:   Creating a datasheet form

Here's how	Here's why
1 Select **tblOrder**	In the Navigation Pane.
2 Click the **Create** tab	
3 In the Forms group, click **Form**	A form opens in Layout view. Because tblOrder has a one-to-many relationship with tblOrderItem, Access inserts tblOrderItem into the form as a datasheet.
4 Save the form as **frmOrderDetails**	
5 Resize the text boxes in the top section of the form	Make them half their original size.
6 Resize the datasheet	Select the datasheet and drag the right border to fit the displayed fields.
7 Change the title to **Orders and Details**	The form should now resemble Exhibit 4-2.
8 Update and close the form	

Subforms

Explanation

You can create a subform by inserting one form into another form. A subform, shown in Exhibit 4-3, can be useful when related data is stored in separate tables and you want to be able to see both sets of data on the same form.

You can create a subform by using the Form Wizard, located on the Create tab, or by dragging one form into another form. To create a subform by dragging:

1   Open a form, in Design view, that will act as the main form.
2   From the Navigation Pane, drag another form into the first form.
3   Format the subform as necessary.
4   Save the form.

Exhibit 4-3: A form and subform

Do it!   **E-4:   Creating a subform**

Here's how	Here's why
1 Open frmRetailers in Design view	You'll add a subform to this form.
2 Drag **frmSalesReps** onto frmRetailers	(From the Navigation Pane.) The pointer changes to a small icon of a form. Don't release the mouse button yet.
Position the icon beside the **lngRetailerID** field, and release the mouse button	lngRetailerID The Sales Reps form is inserted into the Retailers form as a subform. A label for the subform is created automatically.
3 Select the subform's label	frmSalesReps ⊬ Form Header Click the border of the label to make the handles appear.
Press (DELETE)	To delete the label.
4 Resize the Sales Reps form to fit	Click the border of the subform to select it. Then drag its handles to reduce its width and increase its height.
Reposition the Sales Reps form	(If necessary, select the subform, point to its border, and drag.) To fit it beside the fields of the main form.
5 Switch to Form view	The form and subform should resemble Exhibit 4-3.
6 In the main form, observe the last field	The Sales Rep for Spice World is 15.
In the subform, navigate to Emp ID **15**	(Click the Next Record button in the subform until the fifth record appears.) Sales Rep 15 is Sandra Lawrence.
7 Update and close the form	

Navigation forms

Explanation

Yet another way to display information from multiple forms is to use a navigation form. A navigation form contains a navigation control, which is a set of tabs for displaying multiple forms, one per tab as shown in Exhibit 4-4. With a navigation form, you can make a sort of switchboard or central form menu.

You can also configure the navigation form to display automatically when the database is opened.

Here's how you create a navigation form:

1   Click the Create tab.

2   In the Forms group, click Navigation and choose a layout.

3   Drag forms to corresponding tabs. The default name will be that of the form, but you can rename a tab after it has been associated with a form.

4   Format the form as needed, and save it.

Instead of the first two steps above, you also can add the Navigation control to an existing form.

To set the navigation form to open at startup:

1   Choose File, Options.

2   Select Current Database.

3   From the Display Form dropdown list, choose the form that you want to display automatically when the database is opened.

4   Click OK to close the Access Options box. A dialog box appears, with the message that the database must be closed and reopened for the change to take effect.

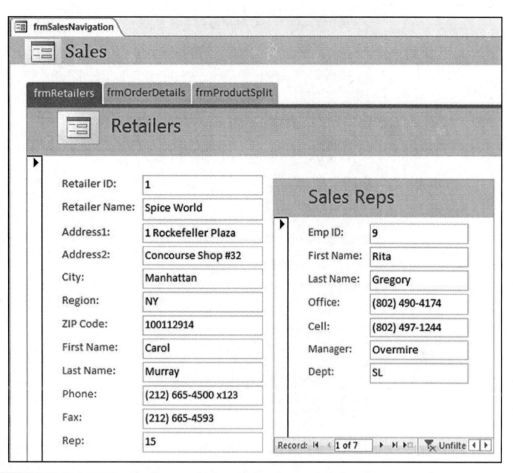

Exhibit 4-4: A navigation form with three tabs

Do it!

E-5: Creating a navigation form

Here's how	Here's why
1 On the Create tab, click **Navigation** and choose **Horizontal Tabs**	A blank navigation form appears with one tab.
2 Save the form as frmSalesNavigation	
3 Double-click the title of the form	(The form title, not the name on the tab.) To make it editable.
Edit the name to read **Sales**	
4 Drag **frmRetailers** from the Navigation Pane to the first tab	A pink bar should appear to the left of the tab.

5	Drag **frmOrderDetails** to the second tab	
6	Associate the third tab with the frmProductSplit and rename the tab **Products**	Drag this form to the third tab. Double-click the tab title and rename it.
	Double-click the title of the new tab and edit it to read **Products**	
7	Update the form and switch to form view	
	Click the different tabs.	The form has three tabs, each of which shows a different form.
8	Choose **File**, **Options**	The Access Options dialog box opens. You'll set this form to appear automatically when the database opens.
	Select **Current Database**	
	From the Display Form dropdown list, choose **frmSalesNavigation**	
	Click **OK**	A dialog box appears.
	Click **OK**	To close the dialog box.
9	Close the database	
10	Re-open the database	The frmSalesNavigation form appears automatically.
	Close the database	For good this time.

Unit summary: Advanced form design

Topic A   In this topic, you learned how to draw a rectangle around a control and change the **tab order** of controls in a form. Then, you learned how to **group** and ungroup controls.

Topic B   In this topic, you learned how to **add graphics** to a form by using an image control and an unbound object frame control.

Topic C   In this topic, you learned how to **bind** a control to a calculated field and create a **calculated control** in a form. You also learned how to align the objects in a form.

Topic D   In this topic, you learned how to add a **combo box** to a form and modify its properties.

Topic E   In this topic, you learned how to create a **multiple-item** form, a **split** form, a **datasheet** form, and a **subform**.

Review questions

1 Name two ways to add a calculated value to your form.

2 How do you align controls in a form?

3 How do you bind a control to a calculated field?

4 Besides using an Alignment option, what is another way to align controls on a form?

5 Which of the following controls is used to add a graphic to a form?

A Image control

B Text box control

C Combo box control

D Calculated control

Independent practice activity

In this activity, you'll add controls to a form and change the tab order of the controls.

The files for this activity are in Student Data folder **Unit 4\Unit summary**.

1 Open RetailersIPA, and then open frmRetailer in Design view.

2 Modify the Form Header section by adding controls as shown in Exhibit 4-5. (*Hint:* Use a label control for the caption **Outlander Spices**, use an image control for the image **Spice_picture**, and use a rectangle control with a 3pt border to surround the label and image controls.) Feel free to adjust this section as you wish.

3 Correct the tab order so that it moves sequentially from top to bottom.

4 Update the form and switch to Form view.

5 Verify that the form resembles Exhibit 4-5.

6 Close the form.

7 Close the database.

Exhibit 4-5: After Step 5, the form should look something like this

Unit 5

Reports and printing

Complete this unit, and you'll know how to:

A Customize report headers and footers, set properties for grouping data in the report, use conditional formatting, and change a report's appearance.

B Add calculated values to a report by using functions, and add a subreport.

C Print database objects and a report on database design.

D Create and print labels.

Topic A: Report formatting

This topic covers the following Microsoft Office Specialist exam objectives for Access 2013.

#	Objective
5.3	**Format a Report**
5.3.4	Add bckgrounds
5.3.7	Insert headers and footers
5.3.8	Insert images
5.3.11	Modify existing reports

Report headers

Explanation

The Report Header section appears on only the first page of a report and is printed before the Page Header section. The Page Header section appears on every page. In the Report Header section, you can include information such as a logo, an image, or a title. You can use buttons in the Header/Footer group to add things like a logo, a title, or the date and time, or you can add these controls manually.

To add a report header to a report:

1   Open the report in Design view.
2   Right-click a section divider or blank area of the report and choose Report Header/Footer to add header and footer sections to the report.
3   Expand the Report Header section.
4   Add the desired controls.
5   Update and close the report.

Do it!

A-1: Adding a report header

The files for this activity are in Student Data folder **Unit 5\Topic A**.

Here's how	Here's why
1 Open Operations1	From the current topic folder.
2 Open rptRetailerByCity in Design view	
3 Right-click the **Page Header** bar and choose **Report Header/Footer**	(Actually, you can right-click anywhere on the report that is not a control.) To display the Report Header and Report Footer sections.
4 Expand the Report Header section, as shown	 Drag the top of the Page Header bar down.
5 Add **Outlander_logo** to the Report Header section	Click the Logo button (in the Header/Footer group on the Design tab), and select the image file from the current unit folder.
Open the Property Sheet	
Select **Auto_HeaderEmptyCell**	 The empty frame beside the logo.
Press DELETE	To remove the frame.
6 Resize the logo frame	 Select the frame and drag the handles.
Change the Size Mode property to Stretch	In the Property Sheet.
Close the Property sheet	

7 Add a label control with the caption **Retailers by City**	

	Click the Label button (on the Design tab), drag to draw the control in the indicated position, and enter the specified text.
8 Click outside the label control	To deselect it.
9 Update the report	
10 Switch to Print Preview	(Click the View button on the Design tab, or click the Print Preview button in the status bar.) To preview the report.
11 Click ▶	To move to the next page of the report. The report header doesn't appear on this page.
12 Close the report	

Report footers

Explanation

The Report Footer section appears on only the last page of a report. In a report footer, you can include details such as report totals and averages.

Resizing controls

When working with controls in the various report sections, you can resize them as needed. To resize a control, select it and drag any of its handles.

Do it!

A-2: Adding a report footer

Here's how	Here's why
1 Open rptProductOrderItem in Design view	You'll add a report footer to this report.
2 Expand the Report Footer section, as shown	◀ Report Footer

3	Add a text box		

4	Open the Property Sheet for the accompanying label control		(If necessary.) Select the label control and click Property Sheet.
	Edit the Caption box to read **Total Amount**		To change the label's caption.
	Close the Property Sheet		
	Resize the label		If necessary.
5	Open the Property Sheet for the new text box control		
	In the Control Source box, enter **=Sum([Amount])**		(On the Data tab.) You'll add the values in the Amount column.
	From the Format list, select **Currency**		
	From the Decimal Places list, select **2**		
	Close the Property Sheet		
6	Update the report		
7	Switch to Print Preview		
8	Scroll to the end of the page		The text box *doesn't* appear on this page.
9	Navigate to the last page		(Click the Last Page button in the navigation bar.) The text box appears between the order information and the date and page number footer. The text box displays the calculated value.

Conditional formatting

Explanation

Conditional formatting allows you to change the format of a field based on criteria you specify. For instance, you can format a field so that if its amount is negative, it will be displayed in red. To set the style, font color, and background color of a field, you use the New Formatting Rule dialog box, shown in Exhibit 5-1.

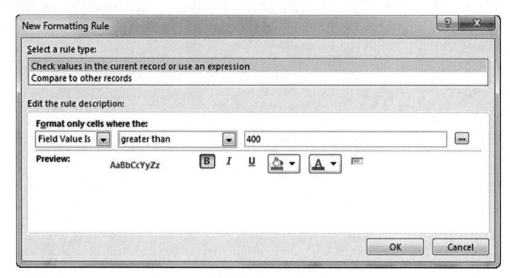

Exhibit 5-1: The New Formatting Rule dialog box

To use conditional formatting:

1   Open the report in Design view.

2   Select the control that you want to format.

3   On the Format tab, in the Control Formatting group, click Conditional Formatting to open the Conditional Formatting Rules Manager.

4   Specify the required conditions.

5   Specify the desired format and click OK.

Do it! **A-3: Applying conditional formatting**

Here's how	Here's why
1 Switch to Design view	
2 In the Detail section, select the Amount text box	
3 On the Format tab, in the Control Formatting group, click **Conditional Formatting**	To open the Conditional Formatting Rules Manager.
4 Click **New Rule**	To open the New Formatting Rule dialog box.
5 In the first list, verify that **Field Value Is** is selected	
6 From the second list, select **greater than**	
7 In the text box, enter **400**	

Format only cells where the:
Field Value Is ▾ | greater than ▾ | 400

8 Click **B**	To apply bold formatting to values that match the condition.
9 Select a red font color	
10 Click **OK**	To close the New Formatting Rule dialog box.
11 Click **OK**	To close the Conditional Formatting Rules Manager.
12 Update the report	
13 Switch to Print Preview	In the Amount column, all values greater than $400 are shown in bold red text.
14 Close the report	

The Keep Together property

Explanation

You can use the *Keep Together* property to ensure that a complete section of the report is always printed on one page. For example, you might want to make sure that the Detail section does not display a portion of a record on one page and the remaining portion on the next page.

To set the Keep Together property:

1 Open the report in Design view.
2 Display the detail section's Property Sheet.
3 From the Keep Together list, select Yes.
4 Close the Property Sheet.

Do it!

A-4: Keeping parts of a report on the same page

Here's how	Here's why
1 Open rptProduct in Print Preview	
2 Set the Zoom control to **100%**	The Zoom control is in the status bar.
Maximize the window	If necessary.
3 Scroll to the end of the first page	Observe that the complete details of Product ID P0007 are not displayed on this page.
4 Navigate to the beginning of the next page	The remaining details about Product ID P0007 appear on this page.
5 Switch to Design view	
6 Open the Property Sheet for the Detail section	Select the Details section and click Property Sheet.
From the Keep Together list, select **Yes**	
Close the Property Sheet	
7 Update the report	
8 Switch to Print Preview	
Scroll to the end of the page	The field details for Product ID P0007 no longer appear on the first page.
9 Navigate to the beginning of the next page	All details for Product ID P0007 now appear on this page, making them easier to read.
10 Close the report	

Group headers and footers

Explanation

Group headers are used as titles when you group a report based on a specific field. You can use group footers to add information such as group totals. You add group headers and footers in the Group, Sort, and Total pane, which you open by clicking Group & Sort on the Design tab.

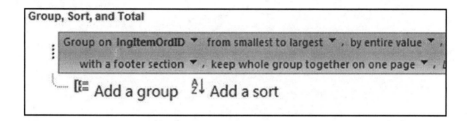

Exhibit 5-2: The Group, Sort, and Total pane (shown in two parts)

Do it!

A-5: Adding controls to group footers

Here's how	Here's why
1 Open rptProductOrderItem in Design view	
2 On the Design tab, click **Group & Sort**	(In the Grouping and Totals group.) To open the Group, Sort, and Total pane at the bottom of the window. A sort by lngItemOrderID is added automatically.
3 Click **More**	To see more options.
4 From the header section list, select **with a header section**	To add a group header to the report.
5 From the footer section list, select **with a footer section**	To add a group footer to the report.
6 From the keep together list, select **keep whole group together on one page**	To print the Group Header, Detail, and Group Footer sections on the same page of the report. The group level should resemble Exhibit 5-2.
7 Close the Group, Sort, and Total pane	

8	Expand the lngItemOrderID Header section	You'll add a label to this section.
	Add a label	Click Label on the Design tab and drag within the lngOrderID Header section.
	Edit the label to read **Order**	
9	Expand the lngOrderID Footer section	You'll add a text box and label to this section.
10	In the lngOrderID Footer section, add a text box control	
11	Edit the caption of the label control to read **Order Amount**	Open the control's Property Sheet and edit the Caption box.
	Resize the label control	To fit the text. Leave the Property Sheet open.
12	Select the new text box control	
	In the Control Source box, enter **=Sum([Amount])**	(On the Data tab in the Property Sheet.) To display the total amount for each product at the end of each product group.
	From the Format list, select **Currency**	
	From the Decimal Places list, select **2**	
	Close the Property Sheet	
13	Update the report	
14	Switch to Print Preview	The total amount appears at the end of each order group.
15	Close the report	If time allows, you can adjust the report's layout.

Forcing a new page

Explanation

You might want to print each set of related data on a separate page. You can do so by using the *Force New Page property*. You can set this property in all sections except for the Page Header and Page Footer sections. You can insert page breaks before a section, after a section, or both.

Do it!

A-6:   Forcing a new page

Here's how	Here's why
1 Open rptProduct in Print Preview	All order information appears together, but you might want to see just one product per page.
2 Switch to Design view	
3 Open the Property Sheet for the Detail section	
From the Force New Page list, select **After Section**	To display each group of data on a separate page.
Close the Property Sheet	
4 Switch to Print Preview	Only the details for Product ID P0001 appear on this page.
5 Navigate through a few pages	Details for each Product ID now appear on separate pages.
6 Close the report without saving	

Page columns

Explanation

You can format reports so that data prints in two or more columns on each page. To do this:

1 Open the report in Design view.
2 In the Page Layout group, click Columns. The Page Layout dialog box appears.
3 Enter the number of columns.
4 Enter the column width.
5 Select a column layout, if desired.
6 Click OK to save your changes and close the dialog box.

Do it!

A-7: Formatting reports in columns

Here's how	Here's why
1 Open rptProduct in Print Preview	You'll split the page into columns.
2 Click **Columns**	(In the Page Layout group.) The Page Layout dialog box opens. The Columns tab is active.
3 Edit the Number of columns box to read **2**	To divide the page into two columns.
Edit the Width box to read **3**	To set the size of each column.
Under Column Layout, choose **Down, then Across**	To display the records in columns instead of rows.
Click **OK**	To save the changes and close the dialog box.
4 Observe the report	The records now display in columns. The header and footer remain centered on the page. The page count is now 2 instead of 4.
Update the report	
5 Close the report	

Background images

Explanation

You can add a background image to a report page. To do this:

1 Open the report in Design view.
2 On the Format tab, click Background Image. The Insert Picture dialog box opens.
3 Select an image file.
4 Click OK. The image is inserted in the report background.
5 On the Property Sheet, adjust the Picture settings as desired. .

Do it!

A-8: Adding a background image

Here's how	Here's why
1 Open rptProductOrderItem in Design View	You'll split the page into columns.
2 On the Format tab, click **Background Image**	The gallery displays the image you added earlier to the header of rptRetailerByCity. You'll use a different image.
Click **Browse...**	The Insert Picture dialog box appears.
Select **Spices-2**	(From the current unit folder.) The image is inserted as a background in the report
3 Open the Property Sheet	If necessary.
In the Picture Size Mode list, select **Zoom**	The picture expands to fill the space.
Switch to Print Preview	The headers and footers use alternating row colors. Since the background image is behind them, they block the image. You'll remove the alternating row covers.
4 Switch to Design view	
Select **IngItemOrdID Header**	
On the Format tab, click **Alternate Back Color**	
From the color picker, choose **No Color**	To remove the alternating row color from this header.
5 Right-click **IngItemOrdID Footer**	
Choose **Alternate/Fill Back Color, None**	To remove the alternating row color from this footer.
6 Switch to Print Preview	The image is no longer obstructed by the alternating row colors.
Update the report	
7 Close the report and the database	

Application parts

Explanation

Access 2013 provides sample databases in the Application Parts gallery. Many of these databases contain formatted reports. You can open these sample databases and view the reports that were designed for them, to get ideas for formatting your own reports. You can also view these reports in Design view, to get an understanding of how they were created. You can also copy reports from these sample databases to your own database. Keep in mind that if you do that, you'll have to reconfigure the report to use your tables and queries, instead of those in the sample report.

To view reports in Application Parts:

1 Choose File.

2 From the New gallery, double-click Blank desktop database.

3 On the Create tab, click Application Parts.

4 Under Quick Start, click Contacts.

5 Click Yes to close the open table and the dialog box.

6 Open and explore the reports in the Contacts database.

Do it!

A-9: Using Application Parts

Here's how	Here's why
1 Choose **File**	To display the File menu.
2 From the New gallery, double-click **Blank desktop database**	A blank database opens, and a blank Table 1 opens by default.
On the Create tab, select **Application Parts**	To display the Application Parts gallery.
Under Quick Start, choose **Contacts**	(To open the Contacts database.) A dialog box appears.
3 Click **Yes**	(To close Table 1 and the dialog box.) The Contacts database opens.
4 Open **ContactList** in Layout View	
Observe the rows and columns used to structure this report	
5 Switch to Design View	
Observe the design of the report	This report uses a page header, left header, and report footer. It also uses carefully arranged labels and text boxes to present information.
6 Close the report and the database	

Topic B: Calculated values and subreports

This topic covers the following Microsoft Office Specialist exam objectives for Access 2013.

#	Objective
5.2	**Set Report Controls**
5.2.3	Add subreports
5.3	**Format a Report**
5.3.2	Add calculated fields

Adding calculated values

Explanation

You can add *calculated values* to a report, and you can display a result that returns a different value based on whether a given condition is true or false.

The DateDiff function

You can use the *DateDiff function* to calculate the difference between two dates. The syntax of the DateDiff function is:

```
DateDiff("interval",[date1],[date2])
```

The first argument is the time interval on which you want to base the calculation of the difference between dates. You can enter yyyy if you want to calculate the difference between years, d if you want to calculate the difference between days, and m if you want to calculate the difference between months. The second and third arguments are the fields that contain the dates. Be sure that both fields have the Date/Time data type. If you want one of the arguments to be the current date, you can use the Date() function.

To create a calculated control by using the DateDiff function:

1   Open the report in Design view.
2   In the desired section, add a text box control.
3   Open the Property Sheet for the text box.
4   Click the Data tab in the Property Sheet. In the Control Source box, enter the expression with the DateDiff function.
5   Close the Property Sheet.

Aligning controls in reports

To align controls, select the controls you want to align and use the appropriate alignment tool on the Arrange tab. You can also use the Snap to Grid option to make it a little easier to keep controls aligned with each other.

Do it!

B-1: Working with the DateDiff function

The files for this activity are in Student Data folder **Unit 5\Topic B**.

Here's how	Here's why
1 Open Operations2	From the current topic folder.
2 Open rptEmployee in Design view	
3 Extend the Detail section	You'll add a control in this section.
4 On the Arrange tab, click **Size/Space**	
Verify that **Snap to Grid** is selected	It's easier to keep the controls aligned if they snap to grid points.
5 In the Detail section, add a text box control under the existing controls	
6 Display the Property Sheet for the new label control	
7 Edit the caption to read **Years at company:**	Leave the Property Sheet open.
Resize the label to fit the text	
8 Select the new text box control	To display its properties.
Edit the Name box to read **Exp**	
In the Control Source box, enter the following code:	On the Data tab in the Property Sheet.
`=DateDiff("yyyy",[dtmHireDate],Date())`	
	This expression will calculate the difference between the value in the Hire Date field and the current date. This expression returns the number of years that an employee has been working with the company.

Reports and printing   **5–17**

9 Select the new label

While holding ⌊ SHIFT ⌋, select the new text box
The Property Sheet displays the properties common to both the label and the text box control.

From the Border Style list, select **Solid**
To apply a border for the controls.

Close the Property Sheet

10 Update the report

11 Switch to Print Preview
The difference between the hire date and the current date now appears in the report.

The IIf function

Explanation

You can use the *IIf (Immediate If) function* to evaluate a condition. You can specify the values that the IIf function should return when the condition is true and when the condition is false. The syntax for the IIf function is:

```
IIf(condition,value_if_true,value_if_false)
```

The first argument is the condition that you want the function to evaluate; the second argument is the value to be returned if the condition is true; and the third argument is the value to be returned if the condition is false. For example:

```
IIf([Amount]>500,"Target met","Target not met")
```

If the value in the Amount field is greater than 500, this expression will return "Target met." If the value is less than 500, it will return "Target not met."

Do it!

B-2: Using the IIf function

Here's how	Here's why
1 Switch to Design view	
2 Add a text box to the Detail section	Place it under the strEmpLastName text box.
3 Delete the label control that was added with the new text box	
Align the new text box under the strEmpLastName text box	
4 Open the Property Sheet for the new text box	
In the Control Source box, enter the following code:	
`=IIf([Exp]>=7,"Senior","Associate")`	
	This expression will return "Senior" if the value in the Exp field is greater than or equal to 7, and "Associate" if it is less than 7.
From the Border Style list, select **Solid**	(Scroll down in the Property Sheet.) To apply a solid border to the text control.
Close the Property Sheet	
5 Update the report	
6 Switch to Print Preview	The new text box displays "Senior" if the employee has been with the company for five or more years; otherwise, it displays "Associate."
7 Close the report	

Subreports

Explanation

You can create a subreport that is embedded within the body of an existing report. A subreport can display data from different tables or queries than those referenced by the main report.

To insert a subreport:

1   Open the main report in Design view.
2   Increase the height of the Detail section, to accommodate the subreport.
3   On the Design tab, in the Controls group, click the Subform/Subreport button.
4   Drag to define the area of the subreport. The SubReport Wizard opens.
5   Select the source (table, query, form, or report) of the subreport.
6   Select a field from the main report and one from the subreport to link the two reports.
7   Select a name for the subreport, if desired.
8   Click Finish to close the wizard. The subreport is inserted in the Detail section of the main report.
9   Edit the subreport as necessary.

Do it!

B-3:   Creating a subreport

Here's how	Here's why
1 Open rptOrder in Design view	This report lists orders for each retailer. The retailers are identified only by their ID numbers. You'll add a subreport to display retailer information with each order.
2 Open the Property Sheet	If necessary.
3 Click anywhere in the Detail section	To select it.
Change the Height to **0.7**	You'll insert the subreport in this space.
4 On the Design tab, in the Controls group, click **Subform/Subreport**, as shown	The pointer changes to an icon of a report.
Drag as shown	

The SubReport Wizard opens.

5	Choose **Use an existing report or form**	
	Select **rptRetailer**	You'll use this existing report as the subreport.
	Click **Next**	
6	From the Form/report fields list, select **lngOrderRetailerID**	You'll link the two reports by retailer ID.
	From the Subform/subreport fields list, select **lngRetailerID**	
	Click **Next**	
	Click **Finish**	The subreport is inserted in the report. Access inserts a label box containing the subreport name. You'll delete this.
7	Select the subreport label, as shown	
	Press (DELETE)	To remove the label
8	Update the report	
9	Switch to Print Preview	Each order is followed by information on the retailer who placed that order.
10	Close the report and the database	

Topic C: Printing

This topic covers the following Microsoft Office Specialist exam objectives for Access 2013.

#	Objective
1.5	**Print and Export a Database**
1.5.2	Print records

Explanation

You can print a paper copy of database objects, including tables, queries, forms, and—of course—reports. For each database object, you can elect to print the entire object or specific elements within that object. For example, you can select a range of records in a table and print only that range.

Printing database objects

To print an entire database object:

1   Select the object in the Navigation pane.
2   On the File tab, click Print. Then click Print on the right side of the window.
3   Select the desired printer and other print options, and click OK.

To print a range of elements within a database object:

1   Open the database object.
2   Select an element or a range within the object.
3   On the File tab, click Print. Then click Print on the right side of the window.
4   In the Print dialog box, under Print Range, select Selected Records, as shown in Exhibit 5-3.
5   Select the desired printer and other print options, and click OK.

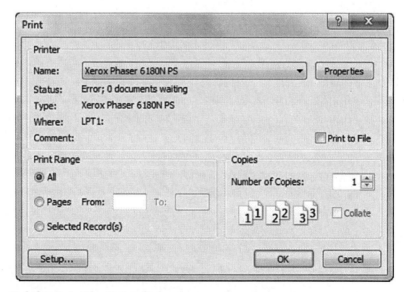

Exhibit 5-3: The Print dialog box

Do it!   ## C-1: Printing a table

The files for this activity are in Student Data folder **Unit 5\Topic C**.

Here's how	Here's why
1 Open Operations3	From the current topic folder.
2 Open tblProduct	You'll explore printing options.
3 Click beside the first row	
	To select that row.
Drag down to Product ID **P0009**	To select all nine records.
4 On the File tab, click **Print**	To display print options. Quick Print would print the whole table to the default printer without further prompting.
5 On the right side of the window, click **Print**	To open the Print dialog box.
6 Observe the Print Range box	You can choose to print All, specific Pages, or the Selected Records.
7 Click **Cancel**	To close the Print dialog box.
8 Close the table	

The Database Documenter

Explanation

You can use the Database Documenter to display and print a report containing your database's design information. You can select the type of database objects and the specific objects that you want to include in the report.

To print a report by using the Database Documenter:

1   Click the Database Tools tab.
2   In the Analyze group, click Database Documenter.
3   In the Documenter dialog box, select the objects you want to include in the report.
4   Click OK to close the dialog box and display the report in Print Preview.
5   On the Print Preview tab, click Print.
6   Select print options and click OK.

Do it!

C-2:   Printing a database document

Here's how	Here's why
1 Click the **Database Tools** tab	You'll print a database document.
2 Click **Database Documenter**	(In the Analyze group.) The Documenter dialog box appears. The Tables tab is active by default.
3 Click the **All Object Types** tab	
Click **Select All**	To print information on all database objects.
Click **OK**	The Object Definition window appears.
4 Point to the center of the page	The pointer changes to a magnifying glass with a plus sign in it.
Click the page	To zoom in on the page.
5 Explore the document	Use the scrollbars and the page buttons on the navigation bar at the bottom of the window to move within pages and from page to page.
6 Observe the ribbon	The Print Preview tab is active by default.
Close the report and the database	

Topic D: Label printing

This topic covers the following Microsoft Office Specialist exam objectives for Access 2013.

#	Objective
5.1	**Create Reports**
5.1.2	Create reports with application parts
5.3	**Format a Report**
5.3.4	Add backgrounds

Explanation

You can create printed labels from database objects such as tables, queries, reports, or forms. For example, you can create inventory labels from a product table, or create address labels from a supplier table, as shown in Exhibit 5-4. The Label Wizard can create labels suitable for printing on industry-standard label stock from over 40 manufacturers.

Creating labels

To create labels by using the Label Wizard:

1. In the Navigation Pane, select a table or other database object.
2. Click the Create tab.
3. In the Reports group, click Labels to open the Label Wizard.
4. Select a manufacturer, and then select one of that manufacturer's label pages. Click Next.
5. Select the font and color for the label text, and click Next.
6. Add fields to the label and click Next.
7. Select a field by which to sort the labels, and click Next.
8. Enter a name for the report and click Finish.

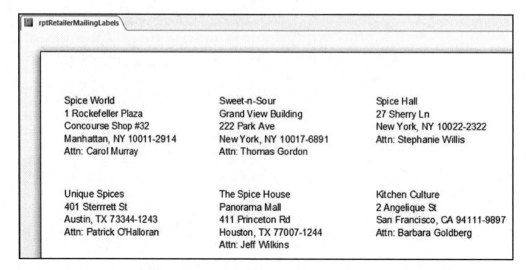

Exhibit 5-4: Mailing labels in Print Preview

Do it!

D-1: Creating labels

The files for this activity are in Student Data folder **Unit 5\Topic D**.

Here's how	Here's why
1 Open Operations4	From the current topic folder.
2 Select **tblRetailer**	In the Navigation Pane. You'll create mailing labels for the retailers in this table.
3 Click the **Create** tab	
4 In the Reports group, click **Labels**	The Label Wizard appears. The first page is used to select the manufacturer and style of the label to be used.
Verify that the Unit of Measure is **English** and the Label Type is **Sheet Feed**	
Click the **Filter by manufacturer** list	To display the list of manufacturers. You'll use the default manufacturer and label product.
Click **Next**	The Font page appears.
5 From the Font name list, select **Arial**	(If necessary.) To set the font.
From the Font size list, select **11**	To set the font size.
Click **Next**	The Fields page appears.
6 Select **strRetailerName**	In the list of Available fields.
Click ⟩	Prototype label: {strRetailerName} To move the field to the Prototype label.
Press ⏎ ENTER	To move to the next line in the Prototype label.
7 Move **strAddr1** to the Prototype label	Select the field, click the Add button, and press Enter.
8 Move **strAddr2** to the Prototype label	
9 Select **strCity**	You'll place the city, state, and ZIP code on the same line, formatted as a mailing address.
Click ⟩	To move the field to the Prototype label.
Press , SPACEBAR	To separate the city and state with a comma and a space.

10	Select **strRegion** and click [>]	
	Press (SPACEBAR)	To enter a space after the state name.
11	Move **strZIPCode** to the Prototype label	
	Press (↵ ENTER)	
12	Type **Attn:** and press (SPACEBAR)	

Move **strFirstName** and **strLastName** to the Prototype label

Prototype label:

| {strRetailerName} |
| {strAddr1} |
| {strAddr2} |
| {strCity} {strRegion} {strZIPCode} |
| Attn: {strFirstName} {strLastName} |

With a space between them.

	Click **Next**	
13	In the Available fields list, select **strZIPCode**	You'll sort the labels by ZIP code for mailing.
	Click [>]	To move this field to the Sort by list.
	Click **Next**	The wizard's final page appears.
14	Edit the report name to read **rptRetailerMailingLabels**	
	Verify that **See the labels as they will look printed** is selected	You'll preview the labels.
	Click **Finish**	To close the wizard and create the labels. The labels appear in Print Preview.
15	Observe the report	The labels appear in the format you created, sorted by ZIP code, as shown in Exhibit 5-4. They are now ready to be printed on label paper.
	Observe the second line of addresses	The addresses for the retailers Unique Spices and Kitchen Culture do not include a second address line (strAddr2 is blank). Rather than print a blank line, Access omits this line.
	Close the report and the database	

Unit summary: Reports and printing

Topic A   In this topic, you learned how to add a **report header** and a report footer to a report. You also learned how to use **conditional formatting** to draw attention to specific data. Then you learned how to use the **Keep Together** property to display a group of related data on the same page. You also learned how to add controls to a **group footer** and how to set the **Force New Page** property to print each set of related data on a new page.

Topic B   In this topic, you learned how to add calculated values by using the **DateDiff()** and **IIf()** functions.

Topic C   In this topic, you learned how to **print database objects**. Then you learned how to use the **Database Documenter** to print a report of the database design.

Topic D   In this topic, you learned how to create **labels** from a table, query, report, or form.

Review questions

1 What is the difference between a report header and a page header?

2 How do you resize controls in a report?

3 Which feature can be used to show negative numbers in a different font and color?

4 What is the function and syntax that can be used to calculate the difference between two dates?

5 What is the function and syntax that can be used to evaluate a condition and return one value if the condition is true and another value if the condition is false?

Independent practice activity

In this activity you'll add a group footer with a Total field to a report. Next, you'll apply conditional formatting to this field so that its content is displayed differently when specific conditions are met. Finally, you'll add a field to a report that displays the difference (in days) between two dates in the report.

The files for this activity are in Student Data folder **Unit 5\Unit summary**.

1 Open OrdersIPA.

2 Display the total quantity sold for each product in the rptOrderItem report by adding a group footer based on Product ID. (*Hint:* Use the sngItemQuantity field in the expression.)

3 Display the data in a different format whenever the Quantity is greater than 200. To do so, add conditional formatting to the sngItemQuantity field.

4 Update the report.

5 Switch to Print Preview.

6 Close the report.

7 In the rptOrder report, add a text box control to display the difference between Order Date and Shipping Date. (*Hint:* You'll need to use "d" as the first parameter in the DateDiff function.)

8 Update the report.

9 Switch to Print Preview to view the report.

10 Close the report.

11 Close the database.

Unit 6
Charts

Complete this unit, and you'll know how to:

A Create and modify a chart in a form.

B Create and modify a chart in a report.

Topic A: Charts in forms

Explanation

You can create a chart in a form to graphically display data from a table or a query. A chart can be either record-bound or global. A *record-bound* chart displays data based on the active record, so it changes each time you navigate to a new record in the form. A *global chart* is based on the whole table and thus remains the same no matter which record you display in the form.

The Chart Wizard

You can use the Chart Wizard to add a chart to a form. Based on the data you specify, the wizard determines whether to display data in a record-bound or global chart.

To create a chart by using the Chart Wizard:

1   Open the form in Design view.
2   In the Controls group on the Design tab, click the Chart control.
3   Drag a box on the form to create a chart. The Chart Wizard starts automatically.
4   Under View, select the table or query on which you want to base the chart. Click Next.
5   Add the desired fields and click Next.
6   Select the desired chart type and click Next.
7   Modify the chart layout and click Next.
8   Select the fields (if any) to which you want to link the chart and the form, and click Next.
9   Enter a title for the chart, select a legend option, and click Finish.

Types of charts in the Chart Wizard

Several types of charts are available in the Chart Wizard, including:

- Column
- Bar
- Area
- Line
- XY (Scatter)
- Pie
- Bubble
- Doughnut

You can experiment to see which type of chart most clearly displays the data you want to show.

Do it!   ## A-1: Creating a chart in a form

The files for this activity are in Student Data folder **Unit 6\Topic A**.

Here's how	Here's why
1 Open Charts1	
Open frmEmployee in Design view	You'll add a chart to this form.
Drag the Detail bar down to the Form Footer bar	To expand the Form Header section. You'll add the chart to this section.
2 In the Controls gallery, click Chart	 The pointer changes to a miniature chart icon.
3 Drag as shown	

To start the Chart Wizard.

4 Under View, select **Queries**

From the list, select **Query: qryEmployeesByDept**   You'll create a chart based on this query.

5 Click **Next**

Add **strDeptCode** and **Employees** to the Fields for Chart list

6 Click **Next**	On this wizard page, you can specify the type of chart you want.
Observe the chart icons	Each icon depicts the type of chart that will be created. A description of the selected chart type appears on the right side of this screen.
Click several of the chart icons, observing the explanation for each one	
Select **Column Chart**	
	In the top-left corner of the screen.
7 Click **Next**	
Verify that the chart layout is as shown	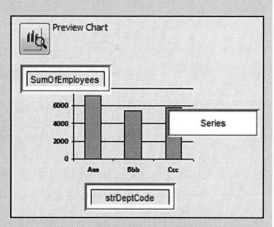
	The X-axis displays the department name abbreviations, and the Y-axis displays the number of employees in each department.
8 Click **Preview Chart**	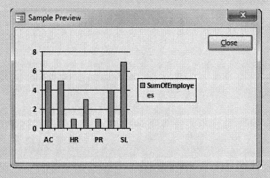
	To open the Sample Preview dialog box. This preview doesn't show how the chart will actually look, but it shows the data that will be charted.
Click **Close**	To close the preview of the chart.

9	Double-click **SumOfEmployees**	`SumOfEmployees`
		To open the Summarize dialog box.
	Observe the options in the Summarize dialog box	These can be used to summarize the employee data.
	Click **Cancel**	To close the Summarize dialog box.
10	Click **Next**	
	From the first Form Fields list, select **<No Field>**	(Scroll up in the Form Fields list, if necessary.) You won't link the chart to the records in the form.
	From the first Chart Fields list, select **<No Field>**	
11	Click **Next**	The last page of the Chart Wizard displays the chart title as qryEmployeesByDept.
	Select **No, don't display a legend**	
	Click **Finish**	To create the chart.
12	Observe the form	The Form Header section displays a chart containing sample data.
13	Switch to Form view	To see the chart with data from the query. It contains the original data and shows the number of employees working in each department.
14	Update the form	
15	Navigate to the next record	Because this is a global chart, it doesn't change when you move to the next record.

Modifying charts

Explanation   You can change a chart by modifying its colors, text, format, and size. You can also add titles for the chart and for the X- and Y-axes, as shown in Exhibit 6-1. To modify a chart, open the form in Design view and then double-click the chart. When you do, the form will open in a separate window, which has a menu bar rather than a Ribbon. The menu bar includes commands for changing the chart type and formatting chart components.

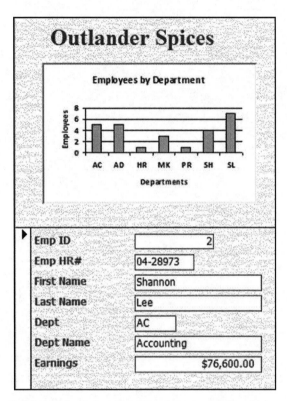

Exhibit 6-1: A form with a chart in the header section

To specify titles for the X- and Y-axes of a chart:

1 Open the form in Design view.
2 Double-click the chart to open the form's Datasheet window.
3 Right-click the chart and choose Chart Options to open the Chart Options dialog box.
4 Click the Titles tab. In the Chart title box, enter a title for the chart.
5 In the Category (X) axis box, enter a title for the X-axis.
6 In the Value (Y) axis box, enter a title for the Y-axis.
7 Click OK.

Do it!

A-2: Modifying a chart in a form

Here's how	Here's why
1 Switch to Design view	
2 Double-click the chart	To make the chart editable. The frmEmployee - Datasheet window appears.
3 Right-click a blank area in the chart object and choose **Chart Options...**	(Don't right-click on the lines or bars.) To open the Chart Options dialog box.
Verify that the Titles tab is active	You'll specify the titles for the chart and its X- and Y-axes.
Edit the Chart title box to read **Employees by Department**	To specify a title for the chart.
4 In the Category (X) axis box, enter **Departments**	To specify a title for the X-axis.
In the Value (Y) axis box, enter **Employees**	To specify a title for the Y-axis.
Click **OK**	To close the Chart Options dialog box.
5 Click outside the chart	(Anywhere on the form.) To exit Chart Options and return to Design view. The chart displays the titles.
6 Switch to Form view	The chart should resemble the one shown in Exhibit 6-1.
7 Update and close the form	
8 Close the database	

Topic B: Charts in reports

Explanation

You can create a chart or graph in a report based on the various groups in the report. To create a chart based on a group, add the chart to the Group Header section of the report. You can also create a chart in other sections of a report, just as you would create them in a form.

Do it!

B-1: Adding a chart to a report

The files for this activity are in Student Data folder **Unit 6\Topic B**.

Here's how	Here's why
1 Open Charts2	From the current topic folder.
2 Open rptEmployee in Design view	
3 Expand the Report Header section so it is at least twice as large	You'll add a bar graph to this section.
4 On the Design tab, click the Chart control	
5 Drag as shown	*Outlander Spices* *Employee Details*
	To start the Chart Wizard.
Under View, select **Queries**	
In the list, verify that **Query: qryEmployeeByYear** is selected	You'll create a chart based on the fields in this query.
6 Click **Next**	
Add **Year** and **Employees** to the Fields for Chart list	You'll create a chart based on these fields.
Click **Next**	The Column Chart layout is selected by default.

7 Click **3-D Bar Chart**

To select the 3-D Bar Chart layout.

Click **Next**

8 Drag **SumOfYear** to the Axis area, as shown

To display the year values on the Y-axis.

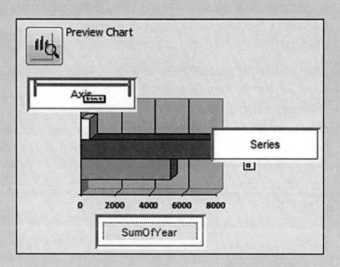

9 Point as shown

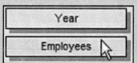

Drag **Employees** to the Data area

To display the number of employees on the X-axis.

10 Preview the chart

Click Preview Chart in the upper-left corner of this screen.

Click **Close**

To close the Sample Preview window.

11 Click **Next**

12 Click **Next**

To display the last page of the Chart Wizard.

Select
No, don't display a legend

Click **Finish**

To create the chart.

13 Update the report

14 Switch to Print Preview

The chart appears in the report, displaying the number of employees hired each year.

Modifying charts in reports

Explanation

You can modify a chart in a report by changing its format, the data on which it is based, or its type. For example, you can change a bar chart to a column chart. To modify a chart type:

1   Open the report in Design view.

2   Double-click the chart. The report opens in a new window with chart-specific command buttons at the top. A Datasheet window displays the values represented in the chart.

3   Right-click the chart and choose Chart Type to open the Chart Type dialog box.

4   From the Chart type list, select a chart type.

5   Click OK.

You can also format the various items in a chart, such as its axes and the chart title. To format a specific area or item in a chart:

1   In Design view, double-click the chart.

2   Double-click the desired item on the chart to open the Format *<item>* dialog box. The name of the dialog box changes based on the selected item. You can also right-click the item and choose Format *<item>* from the shortcut menu.

3   Make the desired changes.

4   Click OK.

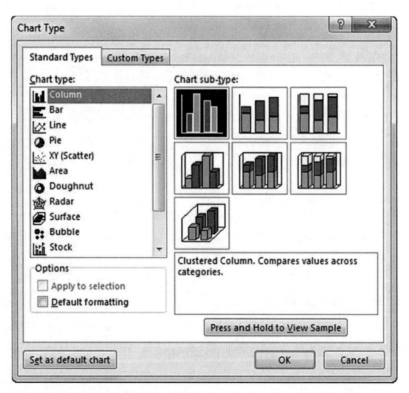

Exhibit 6-2: The Chart Type dialog box

Do it!

B-2:   Modifying a chart in a report

Here's how	Here's why
1 Switch to Design view	
2 Double-click the chart	To open the report in a new window with chart-specific command buttons. The Datasheet window for the rptEmployee report also opens.
3 Right-click the white space in the chart and choose **Chart Type…**	To open the Chart Type dialog box, shown in Exhibit 6-2.
4 Verify that the Standard Types tab is active From the Chart type list, select **Column** Click **OK**	
5 Edit the title of the chart to read **Employees by Year**	Click the Chart Title and enter the new text.
6 Right-click within the white area of the chart and choose **Format Chart Area…**	To open the Format Chart Area dialog box.
7 Under Area, click as shown	To change the color of the chart area to light blue.
8 Click **OK**	
9 Right-click within the Plot Area as shown and choose **Format Plot Area…**	To open the Format Plot Area dialog box.
10 Under Area, select a light yellow color	

11	Click **OK**	The color of the selected chart area changes.
12	Right-click the title and choose **Format Chart Title...**	
	Click the **Font** tab	You'll modify the font style of the chart title.
	From the Font Style list, select **Bold Italic**	
	Click **OK**	
13	Click outside the chart	To return to Design view.
14	Update the report	
15	Switch to Print Preview	To see the changes you made in the chart. It is now a column chart.
16	Close the report	
17	Close the database	

Unit summary: Charts

Topic A   In this topic, you learned how to create a chart in a form by using the **Chart Wizard**. You also learned how to change the appearance of a chart by adding **titles** to its X- and Y-axes.

Topic B   In this topic, you learned how to **add a chart to a report**. You also learned how to modify a chart by changing its chart type.

Review questions

1   What is a record-bound chart?

2   What is a global chart?

3   Name at least two chart types.

4   How is the process of creating a chart in a report different from creating a chart in a form?

5   What is the procedure to modify the chart type?

Independent practice activity

In this activity, you'll create and modify a chart in a form.

The files for this activity are in Student Data folder **Unit 6\Unit summary**.

1 Open ChartsIPA.

2 Create a line chart in the frmOrderByMonth form. Base the chart on the Month and Orders fields of the qryOrdersByMonth query. The chart should not be related to any record in the form.

(Hint: On the fourth page of the Chart Wizard, you'll need to place Orders in the Data area and place Month in the Axis area. Before you do that you can remove the SumOfMonth field from the Data area by dragging it to the Month field or the Axis area.)

3 Specify **Orders by Month** as the chart title, **Months** as the X-axis name, and **Orders** as the Y-axis name.

4 Switch to Form view and compare your results with Exhibit 6-3.

5 Update the form.

6 Close the form.

7 Close the database.

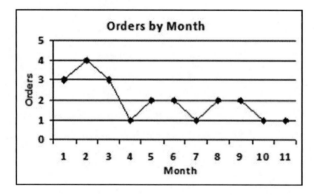

Exhibit 6-3: After Step 3, the chart should look like this

Appendix A

Microsoft Office Specialist exam objectives

This appendix provides the following information:

A Access 2013 Specialist exam objectives, with references to corresponding coverage in ILT Series courseware.

Topic A: MOS exam objectives

Explanation

The following table lists the Microsoft Office Specialist (MOS) exam objectives for Microsoft Access 2013 and indicates where each objective is covered in conceptual explanations, hands-on activities, or both.

#	Objective	Course level	Conceptual information	Supporting activities
1.0	**Create and Manage a Database**			
1.1	**Create a New Database**			
1.1.1	Create new databases	Basic	Unit 2, Topic A	A-4
1.1.2	Create databases use templates	Basic	Unit 2, Topic A	A-2
1.1.3	Create databases in older formats	Advanced	Unit 6, Topic A	A-1
1.1.4	Create databases use wizards	Basic	Unit 7, Topic A	A-3
1.2	**Manage Relationships and Keys**			
1.2.1	Edit references between tables	Intermediate	Unit 1, Topic C	C-1
1.2.2	Create and modify relationships	Intermediate	Unit 1, Topic B	B-2
1.2.3	Set primary key fields	Basic	Unit 2, Topic C	C-4, C-8
1.2.4	Enforce referential integrity	Intermediate	Unit 1, Topic C	C-2
1.2.5	Set foreign keys	Intermediate	Unit 1, Topic B	B-1
1.2.6	View relationships	Intermediate	Unit 1, Topic C	C-1
1.3	**Navigate through a Database**			
1.3.1	Navigate to specific records	Basic	Unit 3, Topic B	B-1
1.3.2	Set a form as the startup option	Intermediate	Unit 4, Topic E	E-5
1.3.3	Use navigation forms	Intermediate	Unit 4, Topic E	E-5
1.3.4	Set navigation options	Basic	Unit 1, Topic B	B-3
1.3.5	Change views	Basic	Unit 2, Topic B	B-4
1.4	**Protect and Maintain a Database**			
1.4.1	Compact databases	Advanced	Unit 6, Topic A	A-4
1.4.2	Repair databases	Advanced	Unit 6, Topic A	A-4
1.4.3	Back up databases	Advanced	Unit 6, Topic A	A-5
1.4.4	Split databases	Advanced	Unit 6, Topic A	A-3

#	Objective	Course level	Conceptual information	Supporting activities
1.4	**Protect and Maintain a Database (continued)**			
1.4.5	Encrypt databases with a password	Advanced	Unit 6, Topic B	B-1
1.4.6	Merge databases	Advanced	Unit 5, Topic A	A-1
1.4.7	Recover data from backups	Advanced	Unit 6, Topic A	A-5
1.5	**Print and Export a Database**			
1.5.1	Print reports	Basic	Unit 7, Topic B	B-6
1.5.2	Print records	Intermediate	Unit 5, Topic C	C-1
1.5.3	Maintain backward compatibility	Advanced	Unit 6, Topic A	A-1
1.5.4	Save databases as templates	Basic	Unit 2, Topic A	A-3
1.5.5	Save databases to external locations	Advanced	Unit 6, Topic A	A-5
1.5.6	Export to alternate formats	Advanced	Unit 5, Topic B	B-4
2.0	**Build Tables**			
2.1	**Create a Table**			
2.1.1	Create new tables	Basic	Unit 2, Topic C	C-2
2.1.2	Import External data into tables	Advanced	Unit 5, Topic A	A-2
2.1.3	Create linked tables from external sources	Advanced	Unit 5, Topic D	D-1
2.1.4	Import tables from other database	Advanced	Unit 5, Topic A	A-4
2.1.5	Create tables from templates and application parts	Basic	Unit 2, Topic C	C-1
2.2	**Format a Table**			
2.2.1	Hide fields in tables	Basic	Unit 3, Topic B	B-3
2.2.2	Change data formats	Basic	Unit 4, Topic A	A-6
2.2.3	Add total rows	Basic	Unit 3, Topic A	A-5
2.2.4	Add table descriptions	Basic	Unit 2, Topic C	C-1, C-3
2.2.5	Rename tables	Basic	Unit 2, Topic C	C-1, C-7

#	Objective	Course level	Conceptual information	Supporting activities
2.3	**Manage Records**			
2.3.1	Update records	Basic	Unit 3, Topic B	B-1
2.3.2	Add new records	Basic	Unit 2, Topic C	C-6
2.3.3	Delete records	Basic	Unit 3, Topic C	C-7
2.3.4	Append records from external data	Advanced	Unit 5, Topic A	A-5
2.3.5	Find and replace data	Basic	Unit 3, Topic B	B-1
2.3.6	Sort records	Basic	Unit 3, Topic B	C-1
2.3.7	Filter records	Basic	Unit 3, Topic B	C-1
2.3.8	Group records	Basic	Unit 7, Topic B	B-3
2.4	**Create and Modify Fields**			
2.4.1	Add fields to tables	Basic	Unit 2, Topic C	C-3
			Unit 3, Topic A	A-2
2.4.2	Add validation rules to tables	Basic	Unit 4, Topic C	C-1
2.4.3	Change field captions	Basic	Unit 3, Topic A	A-2
2.4.4	Change field sizes	Basic	Unit 4, Topic A	A-3
2.4.5	Change field data types	Basic	Unit 2, Topic C	C-3
2.4.6	Configure fields to auto-increment	Basic	Unit 2, Topic C	C-3
2.4.7	Set default values	Basic	Unit 4, Topic A	A-5
2.4.8	Use input masks	Basic	Unit 4, Topic B	B-1
2.49	Delete fields	Basic	Unit 3, Topic A	A-2
3.0	**Create Queries**			
3.1	**Create a Query**			
3.1.1	Run queries	Basic	Unit 5, Topic A	A-4
3.1.2	Create crosstab queries	Advanced	Unit 2, Topic A	A-2
3.1.3	Create parameter queries	Advanced	Unit 2, Topic B	B-1
3.1.4	Create action queries	Basic	Unit 5, Topic A	A-3
3.1.5	Create multi-table queries	Intermediate	Unit 3, Topic A	A-2
3.1.6	Save queries	Basic	Unit 5, Topic A	A-4
3.1.7	Delete queries	Advanced	Unit 2, Topic C	C-2

#	Objective	Course level	Conceptual information	Supporting activities
3.2	**Modify a Query**			
3.2.1	Rename queries	Advanced	Unit 2, Topic C	C-4
3.2.2	Add new fields	Basic	Unit 5, Topic B	B-2
3.2.3	Remove fields	Basic	Unit 5, Topic B	B-2
3.2.4	Hide fields	Basic	Unit 5, Topic B	B-2
3.2.5	Sort data within queries	Basic	Unit 5, Topic A	A-5
3.2.6	Format fields within queries	Intermediate	Unit 3, Topic B	B-2
3.3	**Utilize Calculated Fields and Grouping within a Query**			
3.3.1	Add calculated fields	Intermediate	Unit 3, Topic B	B-1
3.3.2	Add conditional logic	Intermediate	Unit 3, Topic B	B-3
3.3.3	Group and summarize data	Basic	Unit 5, Topic C	C-6
3.3.4	Use comparison operators	Basic	Unit 5, Topic C	C-1
3.3.5	Use basic operators	Basic	Unit 5, Topic C	C-3

4.0   Create Forms

#	Objective	Course level	Conceptual information	Supporting activities
4.1	**Create a Form**			
4.1.1	Create new forms	Basic	Unit 6, Topic A	A-2
4.1.2	Create forms with application parts	Basic	Unit 6, Topic A	A-2
4.1.3	Delete forms	Basic	Unit 6, Topic A	A-2
4.2	**Set Form Controls**			
4.2.1	Move form controls	Basic	Unit 6, Topic B	B-2
4.2.2	Add form controls	Basic	Unit 6, Topic B	B-2
4.2.3	Modify data sources	Basic	Unit 6, Topic B	B-2
4.2.4	Remove form controls	Basic	Unit 6, Topic B	B-2
4.2.5	Set form control properties	Basic	Unit 6, Topic B	B-3
4.2.6	Manage labels	Basic	Unit 6, Topic B	B-2

#	Objective	Course level	Conceptual information	Supporting activities
4.3	**Format a Form**			
4.3.1	Modify tab order in forms	Intermediate	Unit 4, Topic A	A-2
4.3.2	Format print layouts	Intermediate	Unit 4, Topic A	A-5
4.3.3	Sort records	Basic	Unit 6, Topic C	C-1
4.3.4	Apply themes	Basic	Unit 6, Topic B	B-3
4.3.5	Change margins	Intermediate	Unit 4, Topic A	A-5
4.3.6	Insert backgrounds	Intermediate	Unit 4, Topic B	B-3
4.3.7	Auto-order forms	Intermediate	Unit 4, Topic A	A-2
4.3.8	Insert headers and footers	Basic	Unit 6, Topic B	B-1
4.3.9	Insert images	Intermediate	Unit 4, Topic B	B-1
4.3.10	Modify existing forms	Intermediate	Unit 4, Topic D	D-1
5.0	**Create Reports**			
5.1	**Create a Report**			
5.1.1	Create new reports	Basic	Unit 7, Topic A	A-2
5.1.2	Create reports with application parts	Intermediate	Unit 5, Topic A	A-9
5.1.3	Delete reports	Basic	Unit 7, Topic A	A-3
5.2	**Set Report Controls**			
5.2.1	Group data by fields	Basic	Unit 7, Topic B	B-3
5.2.2	Sort data	Basic	Unit 7, Topic B	B-3
5.2.3	Add subreports	Intermediate	Unit 5, Topic D	B-3
5.2.4	Modify data sources	Basic	Unit 7, Topic A	A-4
5.2.5	Add report controls	Basic	Unit 7, Topic A	A-4
5.2.6	Manage labels	Basic	Unit 7, Topic A	A-4
5.3	**Format a Report**			
5.3.1	Format reports into multiple columns	Intermediate	Unit 5, Topic A	A-7
5.3.2	Add calculated fields	Intermediate	Unit 5, Topic B	B-1
5.3.3	Set margins	Basic	Unit 7, Topic B	B-6
5.3.4	Add backgrounds	Intermediate	Unit 5, Topic D	A-8

#	Objective	Course level	Conceptual information	Supporting activities
5.3	**Format a Report (continued)**			
5.3.5	Change report orientation	Basic	Unit 7, Topic B	B-6
5.3.6	Change sort order	Basic	Unit 7, Topic B	B-3
5.3.7	Insert headers and footers	Intermediate	Unit 5, Topic A	A-1, A-2
5.3.8	Insert images	Intermediate	Unit 5, Topic A	A-1
5.3.9	Insert page numbers	Basic	Unit 7, Topic A	A-4
5.3.10	Apply themes	Basic	Unit 7, Topic B	B-2
5.3.11	Modify existing reports	Intermediate	Unit 5, Topic A	A-1

Course summary

This summary contains information to help you bring the course to a successful conclusion. Using this information, you will be able to:

A Use the summary text to reinforce what you've learned in class.

B Determine the next course in this series, as well as any other resources that might help you continue to learn about Microsoft Access 2013.

Topic A: Course summary

Use the following summary text to reinforce what you've learned in class.

Unit summaries

Unit 1

In this unit, you learned how to **normalize** tables, and you learned about the conditions that must be met for a table to be in the first, second, or third normal form. Then, you used the Table Analyzer and identified **object dependencies**. Next, you created **relationships** between tables in a database. You learned about the three types of relationships (one-to-one, one-to-many, and many-to-many), and used a **junction table** to create a many-to-many relationship. You also implemented **referential integrity** between related tables to avoid orphan records. You also set the **Cascade Delete** and **Cascade Update** options so that when a record in one table is changed, the change is also made in all related fields and tables.

Unit 2

In this unit, you learned that a **lookup field** gets its data from a field in a related table or from a list of data you provide. You created lookup fields and **multi-valued** fields. Next, you modified lookup field properties. You also inserted a **combo box** in a text field. Finally, you inserted a **subdatasheet** in a table and used it to enter data in related tables.

Unit 3

In this unit, you learned how to create **queries** using multiple tables. You used the Query Wizard to **join tables**, and you created a query in Design view. You created an outer join, an inner join, and a self-join. You also used the **Find Unmatched Query Wizard** to display the records that do not match between tables. Next, you found **duplicate records** and deleted a table from a query. Then, you created a **calculated field** by entering an expression in Design view and by using the Expression Builder. You also **grouped records** and displayed **summary fields**. Finally, you learned how to concatenate and display the values in more than one field.

Unit 4

In this unit, you drew a rectangle around a control and changed the **tab order** of controls in a form. Then you **grouped** and ungrouped controls. Next, you added graphics to a form by using an **image control** and an **unbound object frame control**. Then, you learned how to **bind** a control to a calculated field and create a **calculated control** in a form. You also aligned the objects in a form. Then you formatted a form for **printing**. You then added a combo box to a form and changed its properties. Next, you created **multiple-item forms**, **split forms**, **datasheet forms**, and **subforms**. Finally, you created a **navigation form**, and set it to be the **display form** that appears automatically when a database is opened.

Unit 5

In this unit, you added a **report header** and a report footer to a report. You also used **conditional formatting** to draw attention to specific data. Then, you used the **Keep Together** property to display a group of related data on the same page. You also added controls to a **group footer** and set the **Force New Page** property. You arranged data in **columns** on reports, and added a **background image**. Then, you added calculated values by using the **DateDiff()** and **IIf()** functions, and created a **subreport**. You also learned how to **print** database objects, a database document, and labels.

Unit 6

In this unit, you used the **Chart Wizard** to add a chart to a form. You also changed the chart's appearance by adding titles to the chart's X- and Y-axes. You then added a chart to a report and changed the chart type.

Topic B: Continued learning after class

It is impossible to learn Access in a single day. To get the most out of this class, you should begin working with Access to perform real tasks as soon as possible. We also offer resources for continued learning.

Next courses in this series

This is the second course in this series. The next course in this series is:

- *Access 2013: Advanced, MOS Edition*

Other resources

For more information on this and other topics, go to **www.Crisp360.com**.

Crisp360 is an online community where you can expand your knowledge base, connect with other professionals, and purchase individual training solutions.

Glossary

Attachment data type

A data type that allows you to attach a file, such as a graphic or other document, to a record in a database.

Calculated control

A control used to add a calculated value to a form.

Calculated fields

Fields that contain values based on the result of calculations performed on other fields.

Cascade Delete

The option that removes records in related tables when you remove a record in a primary table. This option maintains referential integrity and ensures that there are no orphan records in the related tables.

Cascade Update

The option that updates all related tables when a primary-key value is changed in a table. This option preserves the referential integrity between tables.

Chart Wizard

A feature that leads you through the process of adding a chart to a form or report. Based on the data you specify, the wizard determines whether to display data in a record-bound or global chart.

Column area

The area that holds a column field in a PivotTable.

Column field

A type of PivotTable field that shows items as column labels. They are displayed across the top of PivotTable view.

Combo box

A control that displays a list of values for users to select from and allows users to enter a value, in the same way they'd enter a value in a text box.

Concatenation

The process of combining values from different fields into one field.

Conditional formatting

A feature that enables you to control the format of a field based on specified criteria. For instance, if an amount is negative, it will be displayed in red.

Controls

Objects, such as text boxes, buttons, and labels, which you see in many Windows programs.

Data marker

A symbol that represents a data point in a chart.

Data point

A single value that is plotted in a chart by using symbols such as a dot or bar.

Data series

A set of related data points plotted in a PivotChart and mapping to a column field in a PivotTable. Each data series is represented by a different color.

DateDiff function

A function used to calculate the difference between two dates.

Detail area

The area where a PivotTable summarizes data.

Detail field

A field that summarizes values based on the items selected in the filter, column, and row fields of a PivotTable. These fields usually contain numeric data, such as sales and inventory figures.

Drop areas

The filter, row, column, and detail areas in a PivotTable.

Expression Builder

A dialog box used to create expressions for a calculated field or to specify criteria for retrieving records in a query.

Filter area

The area that holds a filter field in the PivotTable.

Filter field

A field that confines the view in a PivotTable to the specified items.

Find-unmatched query

A query that is used to view records that don't have a matching record in another table.

Force New Page property

A property used to print each set of related data on a separate page in a report. You can set this property in all sections except the Page Header and Page Footer.

Foreign key

A field that matches the primary-key field of another table.

Global chart

A chart that is based on the whole table and thus remains the same no matter which record you display in the form.

Group footers

Footers used when you group a report based on a specific field. You can use group footers to add information such as group totals.

Hide Duplicates property

A property used to hide all duplicate values of a field.

IIf (Immediate If) function

A function used to evaluate a condition. You can specify the values that the IIf function should return when the condition is true and when the condition is false.

Image control

An unbound control that is used to add graphics to a form. After you insert an image into a form, the image can be resized but not edited.

Inner join

A join that extracts data from two tables when the values of the joined fields match. This is the default join type in Access.

Input mask

A feature used to define how data should be entered in a field; also determines the type of data and the number of characters that can be entered in the field. When using an input mask on a combo box, you don't have the option of storing the data with the literal characters you specify.

Join

An association that specifies how data between tables is related. There are three types of joins: outer, inner, and self-joins.

Join line

A line that indicates a relationship between tables.

Junction table

A table used to create a many-to-many relationship between two other tables.

Keep Together property

A property that ensures that a complete section of the report is always printed on one page.

Legend

A key that maps the colors of the data markers to a data series or category in a chart.

List box

A control that displays a list of values for users to select from.

Lookup column

A drop-down list of values for a lookup field.

Lookup field

A field that lists values from another field in the same or a different table or from a user-defined list.

Many-to-many relationship

The connection that exists when several records in one table are related to several records in another table.

Multi-valued field

A lookup field that can be assigned one or more values from a drop-down list.

Normalized tables

Correctly designed tables that do not contain duplicate data. Also called normal form.

One-to-many relationship

The connection that exists when one record in the primary table has several corresponding records in the related table, while a record in the related table has only one corresponding record in the primary table.

One-to-one relationship

The connection that exists when one record in the primary table is related to only one record in the related table, and vice versa.

Orphan records

Records with no related record in a primary table. Such records can get lost and take up disk space without being of any use.

Outer join

A join used when you want your results to include rows that do not have a match in the joined table. In this case, the query results display empty cells in the unmatched record.

Page Header

A section that appears on every page of a report

PivotChart

A graphical representation of the data in a PivotTable. You can move fields between different areas, or change the type of chart to get different views of the same data.

PivotTable

A table used to organize, summarize, and compare large amounts of data. You can rotate the rows and columns in a PivotTable to get different views of the same data.

Record-bound chart

A chart that displays data based on the active record and therefore changes each time you navigate to a different record in the form.

Referential integrity

The condition in which all values in a related table have corresponding values in the primary table. When referential integrity is implemented, changes or deletions in records are reflected throughout related tables.

Report Footer

A section that appears on only the last page of a report. You'd typically include details such as report totals and averages here.

Report Header

A section that appears on only the first page of a report and is printed before the Page Header section. You'd typically include information such as a logo, an image, or a report title.

Row area

The area of the PivotTable that holds a row field.

Row field

A type of PivotTable field that shows items as row labels.

Self-join

A query that displays matching records from the same table when there are matching values in two fields. To create a self-join, you need two copies of the same table.

Single-field primary key

A column containing values that are unique for each row in the table.

Subdatasheet

A datasheet within another datasheet. It displays a set of records from a related table.

Subreport

A report that is embedded in another report. Used when you want to display data from two reports simultaneously.

Summary functions

Functions that calculate aggregate values by performing calculations on a range of values. For example, to find the average sales of each product, you must first group the products together and then use the Avg function.

Tab order

The order in which controls are selected when a user presses the Tab key in a form. The default tab order is determined by the order in which the controls were placed on the form. Each new control is last in the tab order.

Text box

A control that is used to enter data in a table. By default, a cell in a table is a text box control.

Unbound control

A standalone control that does not have a data source. Used to display labels, lines, rectangles, and pictures in forms.

Unbound object frame control

A control used in forms to display objects (such as graphics, Word documents, or Excel worksheets) whose data values are not included in any of the tables in the database.

Index